ROUTLEDGE LIBRARY EDITIONS:
ISLAM, STATE AND SOCIETY

Volume 5

ISLAM AT THE CROSS ROADS

ISLAM AT THE CROSS ROADS
A Brief Survey of the Present Position
and Problems of the World of Islam

DE LACY EVANS O'LEARY

LONDON AND NEW YORK

First published in 1923 by Kegan Paul, Trench, Trubner & Co. Ltd.

This edition first published in 2017
by Routledge
2 Park Square, Milton Park, Abingdon, Oxon OX14 4RN

and by Routledge
711 Third Avenue, New York, NY 10017

Routledge is an imprint of the Taylor & Francis Group, an informa business

© 1923 De Lacy Evans O'Leary

All rights reserved. No part of this book may be reprinted or reproduced or utilised in any form or by any electronic, mechanical, or other means, now known or hereafter invented, including photocopying and recording, or in any information storage or retrieval system, without permission in writing from the publishers.

Trademark notice: Product or corporate names may be trademarks or registered trademarks, and are used only for identification and explanation without intent to infringe.

British Library Cataloguing in Publication Data
A catalogue record for this book is available from the British Library

ISBN: 978-1-138-23270-9 (Set)
ISBN: 978-1-315-31161-6 (Set) (ebk)
ISBN: 978-1-138-21601-3 (Volume 5) (hbk)
ISBN: 978-1-138-21604-4 (Volume 5) (pbk)

Publisher's Note
The publisher has gone to great lengths to ensure the quality of this reprint but points out that some imperfections in the original copies may be apparent.

Disclaimer
The publisher has made every effort to trace copyright holders and would welcome correspondence from those they have been unable to trace.

Islam at the Cross Roads

A BRIEF SURVEY OF THE PRESENT POSITION
AND PROBLEMS OF THE WORLD OF ISLAM

BY
DE LACY O'LEARY, D.D.

LONDON:
KEGAN PAUL, TRENCH, TRUBNER & CO. LTD.
NEW YORK: E. P. DUTTON & CO.
1923

PRINTED IN GREAT BRITAIN
AT THE DEVONSHIRE PRESS, TORQUAY, ENGLAND

CONTENTS

CHAP.		PAGE
I	HISTORICAL DEVELOPMENT OF ISLAM	1
II	INTERNAL REFORMING MOVEMENTS OF MODERN ISLAM	29
III	WESTERN PENETRATION OF ISLAM	50
IV	REACTION OF ISLAM AGAINST THE WEST	95
V	SHI'ITE REACTION ON THE WEST: THE BABIST MOVEMENT	110
VI	PAN-ISLAMIC HOPES AND NATIONALISM	120
VII	THE WAR AND AFTER	154
	INDEX	217

ISLAM AT THE CROSS-ROADS

CHAPTER I

THE HISTORICAL DEVELOPMENT OF ISLAM

THE history of Islam begins with the ministry of the Prophet Muhammad from about 569 A.D. to 623 A.D., and has its locus in the south-west corner of Asia, the land of Arabia which was then a little-known territory and one of those outlying parts which had remained untouched by the progress of civilization. In this isolated region it seems indeed that a section of the human race had been segregated at a period when they had reached the neolithic stage of culture, and that from this time of segregation they had been only occasionally penetrated by the richer forms of culture which developed on either side of them in Mesopotamia and in the Nile valley. It seems clear that the isolation was not complete and that there was some penetration, although very little is known of its details : apparently the cultural influences of Babylon passed down the coast of the Persian Gulf and flourished in South Arabia whence they passed over into Africa, and there was some backwash up western Arabia as far as the Sinaitic peninsula in quite early times. In later pre-Islamic times we know that there were two forces steadily undermining the isolation of Arabia, one of these was the system of trade routes by which the merchandise of India brought by sea to Oman passed along by land to Yemen and was then carried up through the Hijaz, by way of Mecca, and so at last to Syria, Egypt, and Mesopotamia : graffiti scrawled by the merchants on the rocks along the route still remain. Muhammad belonged to a family of such merchants, and himself conducted caravans from Mecca to Syria ; by the coming and going of traders along these routes, and still more by the settlement of Jewish colonists at least as far south as Madina, Arabia was being gradually permeated by the culture of the outside world. The other force working in the same direction was the settlement of Arab tribes on the frontiers of Persia and Syria, where they managed to establish colonies at a time when the Parthian and Roman Empires were temporarily in a state of exhaustion and unable to prevent their settlement, but, making the best of things, employed them as frontier guardians in very much the same way as the Normans were afterwards settled in the north of France. We have no reason to suppose that these Arabs were pushed out of Arabia by famine or over-crowding, although the ancient tradition of the breaking of the dam of Arim, which figures so prominently in legends of early Arabia, seems to indicate that methods of artificial irrigation had

HISTORICAL DEVELOPMENT OF ISLAM

been introduced from Mesopotamia, and the Arabs themselves were unable to maintain the great engineering works which had probably owed their origin to Babylonian engineers, and consequently the agricultural colonies in South Arabia collapsed. But as yet all this early history of Arabia is very imperfectly known. The Semitic migrations of history are directly accounted for by the weakening of the military power protecting the settled lands of Mesopotamia and Syria so that it was no longer possible to keep out predatory Arabs whose ideal it was to live on blackmail raised from the cultivators of the land and to protect them from any other would-be blackmailers. In the time of Muhammad these frontier Arabs had been established for some four hundred years; they were partially civilized and had become Christians, but still remained in close contact with their nomadic kinsmen in the deserts behind. Through them a considerable amount of culture, mainly Hellenistic, had filtered back into Arabia, and this culture, partly due to the intercourse along the trade routes, partly to contact with the semi-civilized Arabs settled on the frontiers, prepared the way for Islam.

The work of the Prophet Muhammad falls into two periods. In the former he was simply a religious teacher preaching the unity of God and the doctrines of a future life and judgment amongst the pagan Arabs of Mecca; the teacher of a religion in which he was very obviously under the influence of Jewish and Christian precedents with which he had come into contact during his travels in Syria, and which had penetrated into Arabia; indeed, there were converts to Christianity in his own family, one of whom Waraqa was the first to encourage him in his spiritual ministry, whilst a Christian captive was his earliest and closest friend. In the second period we find Muhammad a fugitive in Madina, the invited guest of the citizens, who made him the supreme chieftain of the tribal federation which formed the city, and as such he becomes the law-giver and founder of the Muslim state which grew up in a city which was a Jewish colony and where the customary law was that developed by the Rabbis of Southern Mesopotamia, with a strong tincture of the Roman Civil code, with which they had been in contact for some seven centuries. Thus in theology and in law Islam rested upon a solid foundation of the Hellenistic culture of the Græco-Roman world, which had, however, filtered through a Semitic medium before reaching Arabia.

Muhammad declared himself to be the Prophet of the Arab race—the teacher whom God sent to bring them a knowledge of His unity and to reveal to them that there is a future life and a day of reckoning in which men shall give account of their deeds here on earth. Other people knew these truths, but the Arabs were ignorant of them and therefore God sent them His messenger to instruct them in these things. It was part of his mission also to unite the Arab tribes in a fraternity of peace with ordered laws and mutual duties; a brotherhood in which the wealthy should share with the

HISTORICAL DEVELOPMENT OF ISLAM 5

poor according to those primal instincts which prevail throughout the human race but receive their clearest expression in primitive communities. The empires of Rome and Persia enjoyed settled order and established law ; God sent Muhammad to introduce these benefits amongst the Arabs. But the Arabs were not all willing to accept these new conditions ; the wealthy and selfish tribes of Mecca and the south were reluctant to share equal brotherhood with the poor men of the desert, and so Muhammad, confident that the fraternity of the Arab race was the purpose of God, took up arms against them and made war until they were forced to admit the principle of fraternity and confessed the One God to whom as Eternal Judge they were responsible. There was no intention in the days of the Prophet or his early successors of carrying the religion of Islam beyond the Arabs, nor of enrolling non-Arab converts in that religion. Nothing can be more absurd than to picture the early Muslims as religious fanatics who poured out of Arabia to give the alternative of Qur'an or the sword to those whom they conquered. They did thus approach the settled Arabs of the Syrian and Persian frontiers because they were fellow Arabs, and the claim was that all Arabs must unite in the fraternity of Islam, though those who were already Christian were not compelled to renounce their religion—they already confessed the One God so there was no necessity—but when the frontier Arabs were attacked the powers of Byzantium and Persia were compelled to come to their relief and thus, quite unexpectedly the Muslims were drawn into war with those two great empires, and even more unexpectedly, defeated them When once their weakness was thus revealed it was impossible to restrain Arab adventurers from plundering excursions, and these led to the final downfall of Persia and Egypt, in each case the Arabs acting in defiance of the strict orders of the Khalif 'Umar, who did his utmost to check their enterprises, and viewed the results with the greatest alarm and dislike. In these feelings he had with him all the " Old Believers," the surviving companions and closer followers of the Prophet ; but these were far outnumbered by the later converts who had not accepted Islam until they had been forced to do so, and who were never deeply attached to it as a religion but were aroused to make the most of the wonderful opportunities which the sudden and astonishing collapse of the armed forces of Persia and Byzantium, which had hitherto restrained their brigandage, now opened before them. To these new conditions Islam had to adjust itself, but it remained essentially the religion of the Arabs. As formulated by the second Khalif 'Umar the revised position was that the Muslim Arabs were to rule as overlords the lands they had conquered, living on the tribute paid them by the cultivators, who were to retain their own religion, but were to be permanently excluded from Arabia itself. If any of the conquered population embraced Islam they came forthwith free from payment of tribute but liable to

HISTORICAL DEVELOPMENT OF ISLAM

military service and acquired the right to share in the distribution of the spoils of war, and by adopting Islam became Arabs and were enrolled in an Arab tribe. Such adopted tribesmen were technically called *mawlawi*. It is hardly necessary to remind ourselves that in primitive communities adoption invariably ranks as equivalent to blood kinship ; in early Israel participation in the Sacrament of the Passover made an alien an Israelite, and similar parallels appear in the system of all early social groups. Thus Islam remained substantially an Arab religion and, apparently, every discouragement was put in the way of conversion. Every convert meant a loss of tribute to the ruling Arabs and a new claimant to share in the spoils of war ; whilst on the convert's side it meant the loss of all share in the property of his family and liability to military service for which the agricultural population of Syria and Persia had no inclination. In theory nothing could have been better devised than the constitution of 'Umar to preserve the primitive type of Islam, but like every theoretical constitution it broke down in competition with the human weaknesses of those who had to put it into practice. The Arab overlords were not content with the fixed tribute and could not resist the temptation to own and cultivate estates. The loss of revenue from conversions was so serious that, in spite of protests, tribute was levied even from those who had embraced Islam. In fact, within ten years from the Prophet's death, by the conquest of great and wealthy provinces,

Islam was faced with conditions which had never been contemplated and the attempt to reconstruct it so as to preserve the original purpose under these new conditions, was too artificial to last. History makes it clear, however, that the legend of fanatical Muslims sweeping through the world and forcing Islam at the point of the sword upon conquered races, is one of the most fantastically absurd myths that historians have ever repeated. There are plenty of instances of such fanaticism and forced conversion, but these do not belong to the early history of Islam nor to that of the Arabs; those stories come from the banks of the Niger, from the Sudan, and from Sumatra, and are connected with Muslim religious revivals of later days and dubious orthodoxy.

Of Islam, as of Christianity, it is true that corruption began with success; the spiritual ideal ever suffers from the material prosperity acquired by its maintainers, and it is generally admitted that when the leadership of Islam passed into the hands of Mu'awiya, the chieftain of the wealthy clan of the 'Umayyads of the Quraysh tribe who had settled in Syria, the early Islam of the Prophet and his companions suffered eclipse. From this period on, like every other religion, it shows alternating periods of decadence and reform, which are indeed the necessary conditions of the physiological life of a social community. The history of Islam may be divided into three main periods: (i.) In the first we have a ruling Arab aristocracy, intoxicated by its sudden accession to wealth, ruling very inefficiently over a conquered population very much in advance of it in culture ; it forms an Arab period which is only superficially Muslim. (*ii.*) This is succeeded by a period during which the Khalifate remained Arab, but Persian influence was in the ascendancy and Muslim theology and law developed under purely Persian influence, and at last Persian rulers practically controlled Islam in which the Khalifate was little more than a pageant. Finally (*iii.*) this predominance of the Persians was replaced by that of the Turks under whom Islam hardened and took the form which it has at the present time.

(*i.*) During the first period, which extended from the foundation of the 'Umayyad dynasty by Mu'awiya in A.H. 41 (=A.D. 661) to the downfall of the dynasty in A.H. 132 (=A.D. 749) Islam was under the supremacy of a ruling class of Arabs whose heads were turned by their sudden accession to vast wealth and political power, and who, for the most part, were not sincere, or at least, not very earnest Muslims. During this period the real spiritual life of Islam centred more or less in the elements which were disaffected towards the ruling Khalifate, or even in open revolt against it, and thus it was the period during which the sectarian divisions of Islam appear. These show two divergent tendencies, the one a revolt of the conquered Persians who, conscious of a more fully developed culture than the Arabs, evolved a type of Islam which inclined towards mysticism and incorporated many ideas familiar to the older religious life of Persia but alien to Muslim doctrine ; this Persian or Shi'ite schism itself split up into various subdivisions, the more extreme sections hardly claiming to be Muslim, but all showing the same mystic tendencies and a curious fascination for the doctrine of God incarnate in human form, a doctrine which has no place in orthodox Islam. The other revolt is rather associated with those Arabs who were discontented with the secularisation of Islam under the ' Umayyads and craved for the older conditions which had prevailed under the first four Khalifs. In a sense they were the truer representatives of primitive Islam, but they were unlettered desert men and expressed their position so crudely and became so violent and unreasonable in the way they maintained it that Islam generally discarded them. The former group, the Shi'ites, still exist in considerable numbers estimated at 15,000,000, of which rather more than half belong to the sect of " Twelvers," that is to say the adherents of the twelve Imams of whom 'Ali, the Prophet's cousin and son-in-law was the first, and then eleven others in hereditary descent to Muhammad al-Muntazir, who succeeded in A.H. 260 (=A.D. 873) and forthwith " disappeared," his followers believing that he remains in concealment because of the evil days, and will, in due course, return to establish a rule of righteousness on earth. In the meantime, any earthly ruler, such as the Shah of Persia, can at most act as his temporary vicegerent. None of the Shi'ites, of course, recognise the leadership of the Kalif, who is, in their eyes, a usurper and the successor of usurpers who tried to exclude 'Ali from the Imamate and succeeded in excluding his descendants. But different Shi'ite sects differ as to the transmission of the Imamate in the descent from 'Ali. The " Seveners " accept only the first six and then the elder son of the sixth, whom the " Twelvers " believe to have been deprived of his rights. It is amongst the offshoots of the " Seveners " that the wildest sects and those most removed from orthodox Islam appear. Many of these extremer sects exist as secret societies. Of the more moderate groups we have the Zaydites in South Arabia with headquarters at San'a, and the Muslims of Morocco who differ little from the orthodox beyond rejecting the supremacy of the Khalif and following their own system of canon law. All these Shi'ite sects agree in regarding the leadership of Imamate of Islam as vested in the family of 'Ali, the extremer sects going so far as to suppose that 'Ali was the divinely appointed redeemer of mankind, the incarnation of the Holy Spirit, and that the Prophet Muhammad was merely the spokesman of 'Ali; nearly all, save perhaps the Shi'ites of Morocco, attribute a supernatural character to 'Ali and his successors. This strictly legitimist theory, and still more, the doctrine of a divine incarnation, is quite alien to orthodox Islam and reproduces religious ideas which flourished in Persia before the Muslim conquest and which have persisted. Shi'ism is predominant in Persia and in Mesopotamia outside the towns, and it has steadily gained over the Arab tribes which have passed east of the Euphrates.

The other sectaries, known as *Kharijites* or "seceders" were the advocates of free election in the appointment of a leader, but did not regard any earthly head as essential to the existence of Islam, whilst on the theological side they were reactionary—out of touch with the intellectual development of Muslim doctrine; puritans of the most rigid type, and may perhaps be regarded as the true representatives of early Islam. Admittedly they adhered to the earlier standards of life and conduct when the rest of Islam was falling under a luxurious and alien culture.

To-day the Kharijites are directly represented in 'Uman, in East Africa, in the Sahara, and in Algeria. These three latter are comparatively small and isolated communities, interesting survivals of an ancient controversy, but 'Uman is an important state. The particular sect in 'Uman is known as *Ibadi*, after one 'Abdullah ibn Ibad, who settled there under the later 'Umayyads. As Kharijites the people of 'Uman are, of course, regarded as heretics by the generality of Muslims, and the general laxity they show with regard to many points observed elsewhere, tend to confirm this criticism. Theoretically they regard it as right to recognise the leadership of any meritorious Muslim if exercised for the welfare of the community, but entirely reject the idea of a Khalif as the necessary head of Islam. The *Imam* or ruler of 'Uman is supposed to be elected and a series of Imams has held sway since A.H. 134 (=A.D. 751), but in practice the election is held by the *ulema* or "learned in the law" and the candidate is selected from the ruling family. The smaller Ibadi settlement in East Africa owes its origin to intercourse with 'Uman in the tenth century A.D. As it was situated in what was until recently German East Africa, it received very careful attention from German orientalists, and it seems clear that, in the course of time, the Ibadites have assimilated to the general body of the orthodox save that, of course, they do not recognise the Khalif or consider that any Khalif is necessary, and are somewhat slack in various external observances proper to a Muslim. The other Ibadite settlements in Africa have come under French observation since 1882, when they were incorporated in French territory. According to the accounts given by French orientalists, these Ibadis are Muslims of a rigidly puritanical type and resemble the Wahhibis in their theology. The Wahhibis indeed have no historical connection with the Kharijites but owe their origin to somewhat similar influences, namely to the reaction of the non-progressive desert type against the religion and social condition of the settled Arabs, which have been largely corrupted by alien influences. It is a curious point that almost all of these Ibadis are great travellers—the people of 'Uman as seamen, the Algerian Ibadis as travelling merchants—but all keep aloof from intermarriage with Muslims not of their own sect.

It is a common western notion to imagine that the world of Islam can be managed by manipulation of the Sultan of Turkey as Khalif, under the supposition that he is a kind of high priest whom no devout Muslim will venture to disobey. To begin with, every sect which has split off from Islam agrees in repudiating the Khalif; he holds sway only over the Sunni Muslims, and even of these the theoretically orthodox, every vigorous and reforming body of the puritanical reformation, ignores him though they, and presumably even the Kharijites, might rally to his support in defence of Islam against the infidel. This, almost incredible result, has been very nearly achieved by the intense dislike and fear inspired by the western nations, and more particularly the British, during recent years.

During the Arab period the Sunni community, that is to say those who were in communion with the official Khalif, was being permeated by Hellenistic influences which involved speculation in philosophy and theology. Muslim theology does not really develop until the 'Umayyads have passed away, but when it does appear it is clear that the intellectual life of Islam has been permeated by Hellenistic philosophical speculation in the form already made familiar by Christian theology. Towards the end of that period the world of Islam was in some respects in a position similar to that in which it finds itself to-day. Muslims were in touch with a fully developed intellectual activity and scientific thought, and were faced with the problem of how to adopt their own religious beliefs to the demands of contemporary science.

(*ii.*) The Persian period which opened with the accession of the 'Abbasids in A.H. 132 (=A.D.749) saw the overthrow of the Arab aristocracy which had rendered itself odious by its tyranny and rapacity, although the Arab Khalifate was retained. Those who engineered the revolt appealed to the diverse national elements which were anti-Arab, and to the peculiar tenets of the different sects. The indifference of the ruling Arabs to matters of religion was notorious, and the sympathies of the devout were enlisted by the hope of a new and reformed Khalifate, which would be loyal to the principles of Islam. Many promises and pledges were made which never could be kept, and were not meant to be kept. What actually happened was that the Khalifate passed to a section of the Hashimite clan, to which the Prophet himself had belonged, of the tribe of Kuraysh. The main strength of the revolt had been in the Persians, who were largely, though not exclusively, Shi'ites. Many of these expected an hereditary Khalifate in the house of 'Ali, but Islam was not prepared for the full recognition of Shi'ite theories. The 'Abbasids were Arabs, but their sympathies were with the Persians who had elevated them to the Khalifate. Everywhere Persian ministers and officials replaced Arabs, the court was predominantly Persian, and Arab birth exposed a man to freely-expressed hostility and ridicule. A whole movement, known as the Shu'ubiyya, grew up and produced a considerable literature devoted to anti-Arab propaganda. The Arabs were described as semi-savages, ignorant, rapacious, and without religion, boasting of noble descent when their families were but upstarts of yesterday when compared with the noble families of Persia.

The most extraordinary feature of this anti-Arab outburst was that it produced the golden age of Arabic prose literature and scholarship, of canon law and theology, substantially the work of Persians who had learned Arabic, in many cases, late in life, and who were mostly converts to Islam, or the sons of converts.

Under the early 'Abbasids the capital was removed to Mesopotamia and was finally settled in the newly-founded city of Baghdad. The whole of that area was profoundly influenced by Syriac culture, which was simply an orientalised version of later Hellenism. The first eighty years of 'Abbasid rule saw a great intellectual ferment in Islam, due to the application of Greek science and critical enquiry to the traditional theology. In some of the Shi'ite sects this was carried to great length, and the sixth Imam Ja'far as-Sadiq (d. A.D. 765) was especially noted as a student of Greek science and by many regarded as a rationalist. Within the borders of the Sunni community there was a movement whose followers were known us *Mu'tazilites*, who took a semi-rationalistic view of Muslim theology, which was in reality an adaptation of neo-Platonism to Islam : they accepted the Qur'an, but regarded it as created by God and not the uncreated Word which was co-eternal with God, for this, they considered, elevated it to the position of a second person of the Deity; and they rejected the stricter doctrine of determinism prevalent in Islam, for, they said, man could not be justly rewarded or punished for his acts unless he were free to do or not to do. In both these controversies, and in their general teaching as to the person of God, they show plain traces of Hellenistic influence, and indeed retrace some of the most familiar discussions of later Platonism and of Christianity. Unfortunity the Khalif al-Ma'mun (A.D. 813-833) was the devoted adherent of these Mu'tazilites and started an active persecution of those who disagreed with them. Islam had never contemplated the Khalif as an authorised teacher of religion: on matters of theology his opinion was worth neither more nor less than that of any other Muslim, that is to say, it would be worth a great deal if he were learned in the law, worth very little if he were not. "Authority" in religion is understood only in the sense in which an expert is authoritative in dealing with his special subject and owes nothing to official position. There is no priesthood in Islam, and no kind of ordination or university degree carries the prestige which reputation for wisdom alone confers, and which must be ever ready to defend itself. The Khalif al-Ma'mun made a fatal error when he tried to enforce Mu'tazilite doctrine by the aid of the secular arm. There was widespread resistance; those who suffered were honoured as martyrs and saints, and the Mu'tazilite system was utterly discredited by the attempt, and finally collapsed.

In quite recent times some of the liberal Muslims of India have revived the name and call themselves Muʻtazilites: like their predecessors they are seeking to combine the theology of Islam with the teachings of contemporary science, but they have no historical connection with those earlier liberals. Unfortunately the reaction against the Muʻtazilite movement brought Hellenistic studies into discredit and helped towards reaction. As yet, however, there was no restriction upon freedom of thought save in so far as resulted from accepting the Qur'an as a literally inspired revelation. Real freedom must, of course, face the fact that reactionary and obscurantist views have as much right to expression as any others, and that without such expression there can be no full discussion and consequent progress.

The Shiʻites at that time represented the more intellectual and progressive side of Islam, and it was at the courts of Shiʻite princes and under their protection that the philosophers of the Muslim world generally found encouragement and protection. This had an unfortunate result in helping the suspicion that philosophy tended to heresy. To some extent, no doubt, the idea was well founded. The earlier philosophers sincerely believed in the inspiration of the Qur'an and of Aristotle, and tried to combine them in one system of theology; their successors, with a better knowledge of philosophy, were compelled to recognise that such a combination was not practicable and tended to accept the philosopher as the final truth and admit the Qur'an only as a revelation devised for the simple-minded, who were unable to understand the deep truths of philosophy. These ideas provoked the resistance of the orthodox, and about A.H. 232 (=A.D. 846) there began a definite reaction which led to the banning of Greek science in the Sunni communion which was in touch with the Khalifate of Baghdad. It was this reaction against philosophy in the east which led to the rise of a philosophical school in Spain, which, though Sunni, was not in communion with Baghdad but had its own Khalif at Corduba.

The reactionary movement was associated with the decay of the Khalifate, though this was merely an accidental connection. The decay was the natural disintegration which invariably tends to take place in any feudal community, and feudalism was the traditional condition of every oriental state. The essence of feudalism is the delegation of power; the supreme ruler acts only through provincial representatives; whether appointed officials or hereditary nobles is a detail of minor importance. they act through subordinate local officers, and so on, each sharing a delegate part of the jurisdiction of the power above. It shows a series of gradations, each responsible to its immediate superior, and the central authority in contact only with a certain number of the greater officials. Such had been the system in Persia before the Muslim conquest, and it was taken over by the Arabs as a part of the machinery of state. The more thorough-going feudalism of Persia prevailed rather than the comparatively centralised

Byzantine system, no doubt because conquest had brought all the state administration and officials into the hands of the Arabs in Persia, whilst it was only certain provinces and not the central government which came under their control in the case of the Byzantine Empire. The ever-present peril of feudalism is that the delegated authority may be turned into an independent one; the feudal official is practically in the position of a tributary prince, and the relaxation of central control necessarily results in devolution and consequent disintegration.

Under the Khalifs the breaking-up process began in the ninth century A.D., and was most marked in Persia. First the ruling princes of the remoter provinces of Eastern Persia became semi-independent and hereditary; then with the rise of the Buwayhids, who claimed descent from the ancient kings of Persia, the whole power of the Khalif suffered eclipse. The Buwayhids established themselves as an independent dynasty in A.D. 932 and soon afterwards captured Baghdad and administered the temporal power to the Khalifs. The Khalif retained his rank and honoured position, and every act of state was done in his name, but in reality he was only a figure-head maintained as a state symbol. Strangely enough these Buwayhids were Shi'ites and so did not themselves recognise the authority of the Khalif, whom they used as their tool and in whose name they ruled the Muslim world.

(*iii.*) The anti-Persian development came from

the introduction of the Turks as a new and vigorous force from Central Asia. They first came into the Muslim world as mercenaries and slaves in the employ of the Persian rulers. Before long they were converted to Islam, but did not, as a rule, join the Shi'ite sect; on the contrary, they embraced the strictest form of orthodox Muslim teaching as it flourished in the more reactionary Sunni circles. The first important Turkish power was founded in the second half of the tenth century A.D. in the debatable land between Persia and India with its centre at Ghazna in the mountainous Ghor district. Theoretically it was a branch of the principality of the Samanids of Khurasan (A.D. 874-999), its founder Alptakin being a fugitive general in the employ of the Samanids. In 999 A.D. Mahmud, who then occupied the throne of Ghazna, declared his independence of the Samanid princes and was recognised as an independent sovereign by the Khalif of Baghdad; he assumed the title of Sultan, which afterwards became a favourite one with the Turkish rulers. In religion Mahmud of Ghazna shows the fiercely orthodox and reactionary type which afterwards became characteristic of the Turk. Already in Mahmud's time the Saljuq Turks, another and rival branch of his own race, had begun breaking across the Persian frontier and early in the eleventh century migrated in great numbers, cutting off the dominions of Ghazna from the main body of the Khalif's dominions. They had accepted Islam about the middle of the tenth century, and took the same rigidly orthodox position as Mahmud. Under the leadership of Tughril, after Mahmud was dead, they established themselves as a power in Persia, and the Khalif al-Qa'im appealed to them to deliver him from the Buwayhids.

Thus invited, Tughril and his Turks marched west and in A.H. 447 (=A.D. 1055) defeated the Buwayhids and restored, at least in appearance, the freedom of the Khalifate, although in fact they now, under their Sultan, exercised very much the same control as the Buwayhids had done. The Turkish ascendancy to the Khalifate of Baghdad marked a definitely reactionay and conservative change in Muslim culture, at least in Asia. The intellectual freedom of the Persian period had come to an end, and Islam took the non-progressive and narrow attitude which has been characteristic of it ever since; an attitude, it must be noted, not necessary or natural, not in itself Muslim but rather Turkish. The main body of Islam as it appears in mediæval and modern times, displays this predominantly Turkish tone, ability in organization and military undertakings, narrowness and conservatism in intellectual ones.

In the thirteenth century came the Mughul invasion, a purely destructive visitation from the east, and their destroying hordes swept down upon Baghdad in 1258 and the Khalifate established there perished. From the ruin of Baghdad an uncle of the last Khalif escaped and found a refuge in Egypt, where he was hospitably received by the Mamluk Sultan of the day (in A.D. 1261) and there he and his descendants lived in state as honoured guests, though devoid of any political power, until 1538.

The Mamluks of Egypt had been able to offer successful resistance to the Mughuls, but the real restoration of Islam at large after the tide of devastation had receded was the work of the Othmanli Turks, originally a branch of the Oghuz tribe driven forward by the movement of the Mughuls. In the course of the thirteenth century these Othmanlis were able to establish themselves in Asia Minor : in 1358 they crossed into Europe, and in 1453 Constantinople fell into their hands and the Byzantine Empire came to an end. Not long after this the Othmanli Turks were able to secure their position as the leaders of the Sunni world of Islam. In 1517 they conquered Egypt and carried off the Khalif Mutawakkil to Constantinople where for a time he was imprisoned, but at the death of the Sultan Selim in 1520, his successor, Suleyman the Great, gave him his freedom and he returned to Egypt where he died in 1538 after bequeathing his title and rights to the Othmanli Sultans, who have ever since claimed to be Khalifs. The validity of this proceeding is very much open to question. The Khalifate is elective and the form of election has always been maintained ; originally the electors were the chief men of the capital city, who then presented the chosen candidate for the ratification of the people at large. Each Turkish Sultan since the death of the last 'Abbasid Khalif, has been duly elected by the *'ulema* or " doctors of the law " of Constantinople. It is clear that this has not been in any sense a free election for no other candidate was eligible save the one who by hereditary right already was Sultan of Turkey. Yet in defence of this it may reasonably be urged that the fact of being Sultan and as such in command of the financial and military resources of the Turkish Empire, put that candidate at such an advantage that no other competitor could be considered seriously ; any way, the choice has been between such an appointment or a merely phantom Khalifate overshadowed by some secular power such as the Buwayhids, or the Saljuq Sultans, or the Mamluks of Cairo. No doubt it is better that the dignity should be in the hands of one who, under the circumstances, holds the chief temporal power in the Islamic world. Now, quite recently, the Turkish government at Angora has decided to revert to the older arrangement and to maintain the Khalif as a purely " spiritual authority " and apparently to rule through a quasi-republican council. The Khalif is not a Pope, and the " spiritual power " in this case means no more than formal leadership, so apparently we shall see once more the Khalif as an honorary official who registers and gives a kind of prestige to the decrees already passed by those who wield the power. In Madina, when there was an election, the chief men were the electors, but " chief men " is rather a vague term, and there was never any satisfactory definition of the electorate. Perhaps the best statement is to say that the election was a choice made by all those who were most influential in the community by reason of age, military distinction, or rhetorical ability, a choice which had to be as nearly as possible unanimous, and these then presented their choice to the community and induced them to ratify what they had done. Theoretically, therefore, election by the *ulema* is as near the ideal as possible; the Islamic world may reasonably be expected to ratify what had been decided by the leading authorities in law and theology. Precedent justified the holding of the election in the city which had been the late Khalif's capital, and this was duly fulfilled by the holding of the election at Constantinople. Thus it would seem that the way in which the Sultans have been elected Khalifs since 1538 has been quite in accordance with the constitutional law. What then did the last 'Abbasid Khalif bequeath to Suleyman? —apparently nothing but a vague sentiment. There was no hereditary right to be passed on; nothing more valid than election could be cited and the 'Abbasids had no claim beyond this save a family tradition which by law had no value whatever. In so far as the Sultans rest their title on this behest, the claim is worthless; in so far as it rests on the serious judgment of the " learned," in whose eyes the command of sufficient military and financial resources to render authority effective ought to carry great weight, it is thoroughly legal and sound. Time will show whether reversion to the older system will be equally satisfactory.

A tradition exists that the Khalif must be of the Quraysh tribe. This, of course, the Sultan is not; he is not even an Arab. But what is the value of this tradition? Certainly it existed in the days of the early 'Abbasids, but that is all. Whether it really was a Prophetic dictum cannot be known, though it received general acceptance and thus has made a conscientious difficulty in the way of the Khalifate of the Sultans, against which we have the consensus of four centuries in accepting Turks as Khalifs, and such consensus is quite equal in weight to a tradition.

A further claim is that the Khalif should be the guardian of the two holy cities, Mecca and Madina, and this the Sultans have generally been. But, on the one hand there have been times when undoubted Khalifs have not held these cities which have sometimes been in the hands of rebels and even of heretics, whilst on the other hand the Sultans have often not held these cities effectively. To say that the Sultan is Khalif because he holds the holy cities, and that his hold on them is proved by the fact that as a Khalif he has a right to them, is as bad an instance of a vicious circle as can be imagined, though an argument put forward quite seriously in recent years. Presumably the claim, in so far as it has any value, means that the Khalif is the one who seems likely to make good his ultimate hold on the two cities; in other words, that no other claimant bids fair to hold them permanently. This is of some importance as at the present time they are in the hands of the King of the Hijaz, or, as he calls himself, " the King of the Arabs " ; but his hold has only been since 1916, and the Muslim world at large doubts whether it will be permanent, or whether it will cease when the King is no longer supported by Great Britain. The general impression is that the erection of a kingdom in the Hijaz is purely a British device to injure the Sultan, and, as an act of interference with the internal constitution of Islam, is keenly resented. If this kingdom were permanently established it might be used to the detriment of the Sultan's claim to the Khalifate, but if the Khalif is to be simply a spiritual-head without forces to hold any territory, that defect is faced and dismissed. So far, however, the King of the Hijaz, although one of the Quraysh and actually holding the holy cities, has made no claim to the Khalifate himself and presumably does not intend to do so.

Some importance also is attached to the possession of certain sacred relics which the fugitive 'Abbasid brought with him from Baghdad and which his descendant passed on to the Othmanli Sultan, chief amongst them being the supposed mantle of the Prophet. But that mantle was only bought by one of the early 'Abbasids from a private owner ; it had never been in the hands of the 'Umayyad Khalifs, and cannot be treated as conveying any very serious claim to its owner

In fact there is no very convincing argument against the Khalifate of the Turkish Sultan except that drawn from the tradition that the office must be held by one of the Quraysh, and this does not stand for much when no one of the Quraysh is himself making a counter-claim.

The importance of the Khalifate has been rather over-estimated by non-Muslim writers. It has been supposed that the unity of Islam mainly depends upon the Khalif. Putting aside the fact that the Khalif's supremacy is only recognised by the Sunni community, admittedly the largest and most powerful section of Islam though only one section out of several, yet the bond which binds Islam together cannot be in the common head whose "spiritual" functions are so extremely circumscribed as is the case with the Khalif. The real bond, and it is a very real one, is the *hajj* or pilgrimage to the "House of God" at Mecca. This involves an annual re-union of Muslims from all parts of the world and from almost every sect with a common series of devotional exercises shared for several days. That, more than anything else, binds together the whole Muslim community and annually renews the bond. Every sect participates with the exception of some few whose claim to be Muslim is questionable, and all join in the religious worship carried out at Mecca. It is not simply a visit to the holy city and its sacred sites, but a visit paid at a particular season and carried out in a series of liturgical forms ; a condition which impresses a sense of common religious life on all those who participate. So long as the *hajj* is observed and shared by all sections of the world of Islam, so long, it seems, the bond of community will be felt.

CHAPTER II

INTERNAL REFORMING MOVEMENTS OF MODERN ISLAM

THE life of Islam seems to have been buried beneath a hard crust of standardised uniformity, laid over it under Turkish ascendancy, and this has seemed so repressive that many have been led to the conclusion that it exists merely as a fossil with the marks of a life now finished. But this is not altogether the case. In comparatively recent times there have been outbreaks of vigorous activity and religious reform, which show quite clearly that there is a very real life beneath the surface. The movement of reform, it is true, claims to restore the earlier conditions of Islam, and so has a reactionary colour, but this is often the case with religious reforms which assume that the primitive form of religion was the purest and best and that the aim should be to return to this and get rid of later " corruptions."

Popular religion has always tended towards saint-worship; in most cases the survival of older and pre-Islamic beliefs and practices. In Persia and India this shows a belief in the successive incarnations of a divine spirit in the human body, and especially under Hindu influence the worship paid to the saint, who is believed to be such an incarnation, is very little short of that due to God. In North Africa also idolatrous reverence is paid to the *murabits* or "holy men," often those of disordered mind, and they are allowed to indulge every passion without reproof; it is even considered as an honour when one of these saints has carnal intercourse with women otherwise of honourable and good repute, and the husband does not, as a rule, resent such intercourse. This very gross form of saint-worship is certainly not developed from the teachings of Islam, nor is it consistent with them; it is the relic of the baser social and religious conditions prevailing amongst the Berber tribes of Africa before the coming of Islam. In Egypt and Syria those grosser forms of saint-worship do not normally appear, but great reverence is attached to the tombs of famous saints, such as that of Ahmad al-Baidawi at Tanta, the scene of reputed healings and other miracles. Almost every village has its saint's shrine, and such shrines receive even more reverence than the mosque itself. For instance, there is no difficulty in the way of a non-Muslim visiting a mosque, as a rule, but a great deal of difficulty will often be made in the way of visiting an adjoining chamber containing a saint's tomb. In the great mosque at Tanta the Christian visitor will usually be kept waiting outside until the doors of the Sheikh Ahmad al-Badawi's tomb are shut, so that he may look in through the barred windows but not enter.

The pains taken to exclude non-Muslims justify one in saying that the Saint's tomb receives more reverence than the mosque itself. All this is a corruption of primitive Islam, and, in the view of stricter theologians, inconsistent with the orthodox doctrine which restricts worship to God alone. In the eighth century of the Hijra (=A.D. 13th century) Ibn Taymiya was the outspoken opponent of these corruptions, and aroused a great storm by his puritan protests; all the orders of darwishes were allied against him, popular opinion revered the saints living and dead whose honours he disputed, and he was attacked, imprisoned, and molested in every way, but through it all held firmly to his protest and did so in a peculiarly offensive manner, for he had a gift of sarcasm and ridicule. His teaching commanded respect for theologians generally recognised that there was a considerable degree of truth in his arguments, but to most he appeared rather as a crank.

Five centuries passed before his work bore real fruit. In the course of the eighteenth century Muhammad ibn 'Abdu l-Wahhab, a native of the Najd, studied and was convinced by his books; copies still exist which have been made by this admirer. In the Najd there still remained a good deal of the spirit of primitive Islam and of the strict puritanical thought which produced the Kharijites, essentially conservative, reactionary, and severe. There the school of canon law in force followed the teaching of Ibn Hanbal, the most reactionary of the four orthodox schools, whose teaching was practically obsolete elsewhere. At bottom it was the old Semitic spirit which we see in Elijah in the Old Testament, the spirit of protest and disapproval towards all foreign culture, towards all " innovation," and intolerance of all that eases the rigour of life to which the hardy desert men have been accustomed. The Old Testament prophet, clothed in the rough garb of the Arab, made his whole life a witness against Jezebel's attempt to induce the refinements of Phœnician culture, and the desert Arab is equally intolerant towards the mingling of refinement and vice which characterises town life. Such feelings find ready expression in religious fanaticism, but it does not follow that they are always the outcome of religious fervour ; to some extent they are even akin to the " class war " which, at least in part, is inspired by hatred towards refinements and urbanities which smooth the surface of life in the classes warred against. But very often such feelings lend themselves to the religious or social reformer who is able to utilize them, and this was the case in eighteenth century Najd.

Muhammad ibn 'Abdu l-Wahhab (died 1787) was a reformer inspired by the books of Ibn Taymiya and, like his master, attacked the popular worship of saints and exhorted his followers to destroy the shrines which provoked honours which were inconsistent with the honour due to God alone. This was the leading feature of al-Wahhab's teaching, but associated with it was a consistent attempt to restore the primitive rigour of Islam, to enforce strictly the daily prayers, the prohibition against wine, which was extended to the " drinking " (*i.e.* smoking) of tobacco, to eradicate vice, and to abolish all kinds of adornment in the mosque, more especially minarets of the Turkish pattern, and other innovations.

Expelled from the town of 'Ayayna as a person liable to cause political trouble by his reforming zeal, al-Wahhab found a welcome at Dara'iyya, the home of the Sheikh Muhammad ibn Sa'ud, who embraced his teaching and reformed his principality on Wahhabi lines. Under Muhammad and his three successors this state became larger and more powerful and conquered the neighbouring countries until, towards the end of the eighteenth century the dynasty of Ibn Sa'ud had established a powerful kingdom in north-east Arabia, in which the reformed Islam of al-Wahhab was the sole religion permitted. Muslims generally refer to the days before the ministry of Muhammad as " the ignorance," but the Wahhabis apply this name to the time before the reformation, which produced their purging of Islam from popular superstitutions. In 1801 a Wahhabi force moved north and destroyed the Shi'ite shrine at Kerbela. Soon afterwards they got possession of Mecca, and in 1804 of Madina, where they pulled down the tomb erected over the grave of Muhammad, for even he, they held, was but a man, and the shrine tempted Muslims to divert to him the honour due to God. Not long afterwards they were able to extend their sway over 'Uman and Yemen.

Turkish control was not then effective in central Arabia, but it was impossible to ignore the growth of so threatening a power when it overshadowed the sacred cities, and the pilgrimage could only be made under Wahhabi control. It was impossible for the Othmanli authorities to submit to this, and obviously unsuitable that the Sultan, who claimed to be Khalif, could only send to those cities subject to Wahhabi regulations. The Wahhabis were perfectly orthodox but did not recognise the Sultan's Khalifate, and indeed regarded him as unorthodox and semi-idolatrous. To check the Wahhabi movement the Sultan sent the Albanian general Muhammad 'Ali as pasha to Egypt, conferring on him the title of *Khedive*, with a free hand to raise forces and undertake military operations in Arabia. From this arose the quasi-independent Khedivate of Egypt which lasted down to 1915. Muhammad 'Ali's first duty was to make a punitive expedition against the Wahhabis and rescue the holy cities from their hands. The expedition set out under the Khedive's son Tussun in 1810, and war lasted until 1818, when the Wahhabis were defeated. This result was entirely due to the superior arms and artillery of the Egyptians who were armed on the European model and with European material. Before the struggle came to an end the Wahhabi state was visited by the Swiss traveller Burckhardt, himself a convert to Islam, who has left a most interesting and valuable record of his journey in " Notes on the Bedouins and Wahhabis " (2 vols. Lond. 1831).

The victory of the Egyptians finally cleared the Wahhabis out of the holy cities and freed the pilgrim road. For a time their power was broken by this defeat, but in 1830 they began to rally under Turki, a son of 'Abdullah, who had led the Wahhabis to the conquest of Madina, 'Uman, and Yemen. A new capital was established at Riyadh, and in an almost inaccessible part of Arabia this new kingdom of Riyadh continued an obscure existence, much of its time at war with the rival state of Jebel Shammar, too remote to be interfered with by the Turkish government, and too secluded to enter into international politics, until 1901, when the Wahhabis, having suceeded in establishing themselves securely, began to reclaim some of the neighbouring provinces and very soon showed themselves a sturdy and formidable power. The revival of the Wahhabis caused considerable anxiety to the Turkish Sultan, and plans were laid to check its possible extension so as not to interfere with the pilgrim route. The first project was to get the Sharif of Mecca to attack them, for it was always the Turkish policy to foment divisions amongst the Arabs and to keep them weak by alternately helping one and then another of the rival factions, neglect of which General Haldane assigns as one of the reasons of the trouble we have had in Mespotamia : in this case certainly the Sharif was more interested in securing the pilgrim route than anyone else ; it was only a century before that the Wahhabis had held the holy cities. In 1910 the Sharif invaded

Riyadh and for a time put a check upon Wahhabi ambitions, but without being able to produce any permanent result. The Turks relied a good deal upon the strategic railway which was being pushed down into Arabia, nominally as a help to the pilgrims, but in reality as a means of hurrying Turkish troops into the country and so bringing Arabia under effective control.

The Wahhabis were perfectly alive to the threatened danger against which they were able to set off the strong nationalist and anti-Turkish movement then going on amongst the Arabs under the leadership of the Sharif; indeed, he was more seriously threatened by efficient Turkish military control in Arabia than the Wahhabis were; the more securely the pilgrims came down to Mecca under military protection the less need to pay blackmail to the tribes and to employ their "escort" for the pilgrimage. The Wahhabi Imam 'Abdu l-'Aziz ibn 'Abdu r-Rahman ibn Faisal al-Sa'ud, commonly known as Ibn Sa'ud, determined to strike the first blow, and in 1914 descended on the province of Hasa, which had been annexed by the Turks in 1871, but never properly reduced by them. This easily fell into the hands of the Wahhabis, and then came the Great War, which, before long, saw the Turks fully occupied in fighting against the Allies. At an early stage the English re-opened negotiations with the Sharif of Mecca, who had already asked for English help for the Arabs against the Turks, but had been refused on account of the friendly relations then prevailing between England and Turkey, but now, under the changed conditions, the English made the advance in asking for the formation of an anti-Turkish alliance, and the Sharif of Mecca was recognised as King of the Hijaz—the British Government has never formally recognised the title he claims as "King of the Arabs"—and in 1915 messages of encouragement were sent to Ibn Saʻud, which were followed by a formal treaty in 1916. As far back as 1866 there had been an agreement between the British and the Wahhabi State, but all that had passed away. When Ibn Saʻud seized Hasa there was some hesitation as to whether a regular treaty should be made with him, but here, as in dealing with the Hijaz, the British Government was held back by the fear of unfriendly action towards the Turks. Soon after the war commenced Captain Shakespear, the British agent at Kuwait, from whence Ibn Saʻud had made his expedition against Riyadh, went into the Najd, but was killed in warfare between the Wahhabis and the united forces of the Turks and Rashid, after which negotiations were continued by Sir Percy Cox. In 1917 a British mission was sent under Capt. H. St. J. B. Philby, who has written a very full and interesting account of his undertaking in his "Heart of Arabia" (2 vols. Lond. 1922).

Ibn Saʻud has established a strong and orderly government in North-East Arabia, by means which, though primitive and drastic in character, are thoroughly efficient. Apparently, trade and travelling are safe, the people live in security, and there is in every respect a great contrast with the inefficiency of Turkish rule. As Captain Philby pictures it, this Wahhabi system is harsh and unlovely, but certainly there is no truth in Palgrave's description of it as with merely a hypocritical pretence of puritanism on the surface. Its influence is spreading back into Central Arabia, and the use of tobacco, which Wahhabi law forbids, is gradually dying out amongst the Badwin tribes (cf. Philby, op. cit. i., p. 281). On the theological side the Wahhabis in the North-East and the Hijazis in the West represent two divergent tendencies, the former following the strict puritanism of Ibn Taymiya, the latter the modified mysticism transmitted through al-Ghazali, and these two are serious rivals in the political life of Arabia. Ibn Sa'ud has done a great deal to promote the study of the theology characteristic of his sect, and has arranged for the publication in Bombay of the treatise of Muhammad ibn 'Abdu-l-Wahhab, which is the leading text book, and of other theological works of the Wahhabi school as well as of Ibn Ghannam's history of Wahhabism. The Wahhabis regard all other Muslims as more or less tainted with *shirk* or polytheism by the way in which they honour Muhammad, 'Ali, and other great saints and patriarchs (Philby, op. cit. i., 294-5) and especially show their hatred of the Meccans, whom they regard as immoral and irreligious. In the external rites of religion they are strictly orthodox, being especially particular in commencing prayer at the correct times, but are careless as to the formal details of prayer, allowing a degree of diversity not usual amongst other Muslims. It is usual for all Muslims to refer to the days before the coming of Muhammad as the " time of ignorance," but the Wahhabis apply this term to the days before the reformation of Ibn 'Abdu l-Wahhab and thus imply that there are not true Muslims outside their own community. They do not in any way admit that the Khalif has any claim to their allegiance.

At the present moment undoubtedly Ibn Sa'ud is the strongest man in Arabia, and it seems probable that the extension of his rule over 'Iraq would would be welcomed, provided that did not bring with it the enforcing of the religious customs of the Wahhabis. That the British Government is rather committed to the King of the Hijaz is simply due to the unfortunate accident which carried off Colonel Shakespeare in the 1915 campaign. But there are some serious considerations to be remembered against making too much of Ibn Sa'ud. In the first place the present strong rule of the Wahhabi State rests entirely upon the one man; we have no assurance that it would continue under others of his dynasty; it has been proved so often that the greatness of the Arab ruler is purely personal, and the organization only works so long as his hand is in control. And again we have to note that the gifts which fit a man for strong rule over desert tribes may not prove equally efficient when that rule is extended to a land with settled cultivators and cities, such at least is the suggestion of past history; the tribes of the Najd are all more or less of one racial and cultural type, but the population of 'Iraq is not homogeneous and we have no idea how Ibn Sa'ud would get on with non-Arab subjects.

In the Najd Ibn Sa'ud has established a strongly centralized tribal federation, and he has himself done his utmost to secure its permanence. With this end in view he began the formation of the *Ikhwan* or " brotherhood " in 1912, an attempt to replace tribal rivalries by the establishment of a social group united in its religious life, and of this the most important result has been the foundation of various colonies in different parts of Arabia where the settlers are all Wahhabis and where their tribal origins are by common consent ignored in face of religious union. On the theological side the *Ikhwan* has been an effort to revive the original aims of the Wahhabi movement. It is absurd to refer to the *Ikhwan* as a kind of dark conspiracy full of dangers for the outside world; it is essentially a sensible and statesmanlike institution with the best prospects for securing permanent order in Arabia, if such a result be possible, by the settlement of colonies whose members will be united in their communal life. In relation to the non-Wahhabi world Ibn Sa'ud has taken a reactionary attitude, and has taken it more or less of necessity; he has been unwilling to allow European penetration of the Najd and has closed the country to missionaries and non-Muslim traders, not so much, perhaps, because of an accurate

INTERNAL REFORMING MOVEMENTS

estimate of the tendencies of modern penetration as by a reversion to the tradition of early Islam as expressed in the "Constitution of 'Umar" and this, no doubt, is inevitable in the case of an Arabian puritan. When, however, the terrible influenza epidemic of 1918-19 raged in Arabia and Ibn Sa'ud's eldest son fell a victim, he himself sent messengers calling for the medical missionary, Dr. Harrison, of Bahrayn, and this missionary then and several times since has been a welcome visitor at Riyadh. This in itself is peculiarly significant as showing that of all mission work that of the medical mission is the most calculated to overcome sectarian exclusiveness.

In referring to the spread of Wahhabi movements outside Arabia we must go back to the early years of the nineteenth century when Wahhabi rule was supreme in Mecca and Madina. The annual pilgrimage causes these cities to be the very heart of Islam and any religious movement there is quickly passed on to the ends of the Muslim world. Amongst the pilgrims in the early years of the nineteenth century was a certain sheikh named 'Uthman Danfodio, one of the Fulbe or Fulani, a pastoral tribe in the Sedan. At Mecca he became an ardent convert to Wahhabi doctrine and on his return to the Sedan he began preaching it to his fellow Fulbe, who were all simple and earnest Muslims, not only as a religious teacher but as a leader striving to unite his tribesmen in the same way as the Arabs of the Najd had been united. His growing power alarmed the pagan King of

Gober, a Hausa state on the Niger, and he tried to put down Danfodio by force of arms, with the result that the Wahhabis broke out in open rebellion and, supported by a large army of converts, attacked not only the heathen states but also those Muslims who did not accept Wahhabi reforms, and finally made themselves masters of the whole of Hausaland. Danfodio's first outbreak was in, or soon after, the year 1802, and he died in 1816. His work was continued and extended by his two sons, and the kingdom of Fulbe remained the chief power on the Upper Niger, a cruel and fanatical bulwark of the reformed Islam, until Nigeria came under British rule in 1900. During the period of their power the Fulbe did much to extend Islam, largely by warfare on their heathen neighbours, but do not seem to have continued to be so active in missionary work since coming under British rule.

Wahhabi missionaries entered India rather later than the Sudan, and caused a very marked revival of religion in the districts about Bengal where the more ignorant Muslims had mingled much with the Hindus and adopted many of their customs, consulting their astrologers, and even sharing in the contributions made to the idol Durga. The greatest Indian Wahhabi leader was Sayyid Ahmad Shah of Rai Bareilli, who was a robber until 1816, then converted, and a pilgrim to Mecca, where he was brought into contact with the adherents of Wahhabi teaching, and then, on his return to India in 1820, made his headquarters at Patna and spread his influence through the Panjab. He strictly

INTERNAL REFORMING MOVEMENTS

forbade participation in Hindu ceremonies, especially the payment of contributions to idols and to their festivals. India, he held, was not a Muslim country but part of the *daru l-Harb* or "land of war," where Islam is on active service against the unconverted heathen, and so the Friday public prayers cannot be used until the time comes that the land is converted. The area of Wahhabi influence was divided into "circles" each under the direction of an agent. Gradually he succeeded in founding a Wahhabi state in the Panjab, and in 1826 commenced a *jihad* against the Sikhs, but the Sikhs made a vigorous resistance and broke up the Wahhabi State in 1830. Some time later the Panjab was conquered by the British. Sayyid Ahmad Shah's work was continued by his disciple the Mawlawi Muhammad Isma'il and his son Dudhu Miyan, who preached in Dacca. The followers of these stricter Wahhabis are now known as *Rafi-yadaym*, but they are a dwindling sect. A more moderate branch was formed by Mawlawi Karamat 'Ali of Jaunpor (d. 1874) who claimed to be included amongst the Sunni Muslims and accepted the milder Hanifite code of law instead of the Hanbalite code which is the usual one amongst the Wahhabis. India, he taught, is not *daru l-Harb*, and so the Friday congregational prayers may be held lawfully: he even allowed offerings to be made at the tombs of *pirs* or saints, but both he and the stricter branch forbid the observance of the Muharram when the Shi'ites commemorate 'Ali and his two sons. This milder Wahhabi sect is known as the *Ta'aiyuni*, both sects are called *Farazi*, the term "Wahhabi" being in ill repute in India and resented by those to whom it is applied.

About 1803 three pilgrims returned to Sumatra deeply influenced by the evidences of the Wahhabi reforms which they had seen at Mecca and anxious to introduce those puritanical principles into their own country. At first they seem to have been simply reformers working amongst their co-religionists, but later on they started a *jihad* against their heathen neighbours and this finally degenerated into a cruel and savage war of conquest. The Dutch Government was compelled to take action against them in 1821, and, after sixteen years fighting, took their strongholds and broke their power.

In each case the immediate and direct result of the Wahhabi movement was the attempt to set up a theocratic state and to propagate Islam by armed force. The movement itself is undoubtedly true to the older ideals of Islam, for saint-worship is not only a later accretion but can be traced in every case to the influence of non-Muslim religions : at the same time it is reactionary in the extreme and essentially anti-Western in its tendency.

The *Sanusi* brotherhood owes its beginnings to Wahhabi inspiration. Its founder, Muhammad 'Ali as-Sanusi, was born in Algeria in 1787 and educated in Mecca. In 1839 he returned to Algeria and founded sevearl *zawias* or monasteries of darwishes in the Benghazi district. Then he went back to Mecca and established a *zawia* there, but

INTERNAL REFORMING MOVEMENTS

his teaching was too much on the lines of Wahhabi doctrine, which was then in disfavour, and he was advised to leave. In 1843 he settled in Tripoli, where, however, he again met with opposition, and so in 1856 he retired to the edge of the desert and established himself in the oasis of Jarabub, which became the headquarters of the Sanusi *ikhwan*, and from thence it has spread out through North Africa and to Arabia and even to the Malay archipelago. In substance, the teaching of this brotherhood is identical with that of the Whahabis, but the brotherhood is organised as a corporate community under the leadership of the Sanusi and with a regular hierarchy of officers on the lines usual in Muslim religious confraternities. It is divided into local *zawias* which may be regular monasteries or simply a kind of masonic lodge, each under a head, who is called the Mukaddam. The brotherhood has been and is noteworthy by its missionary activity and has contributed considerably to the spread of Islam in North Africa and elsewhere, indeed, every Wahhabi body which is due to Wahhabi influence shows a strong propagandist spirit. It is indeed an important proof of the real vitality which is in Islam to-day, but the Sanusi body hardly justifies the alarmist tone which appears in some European writers. On theological grounds the Sanusi very strongly disapproved the claims of the Sudanese Mahdi and assisted the British in their attack upon him. Both then, and since, up to 1914, their general attitude was distinctly pro-British, although necessarily opposed to the introduction of European customs and to intercourse between Europeans and their own colonies, a position arising from their Wahhabi principles. They never submitted to 'Abdu l-Hamid nor recognised his Khalifate, nor joined in his pan-Islamic policy, though themselves working for the union of Muslim Africa and for the exclusion of the alien. Muhammad 'Ali died in 1859 and was succeeded by his son Muhammad al-Mahdi as-Sanusi, a mystic, who held himself aloof from his followers and was in great repute as a saint and as the Mahdi or forerunner of the Messiah, a mystical element which sharply distinguishes the Sanusi sect since his time from the Wahhabis proper, who admit nothing of this kind. It was this belief in their own Mahdi which disposed the Sanusi to regard the Sudanese Mahdi as an impostor and caused them to support the British in their operations against him. At Muhammad's death in 1902 he was succeeded by his nephew Ahmad ash-Sharif, as his son, Muhammad Idris (born 1889) was too young, though he is destined to be the head in due course. The Italian attack upon Tripoli in 1911 changed the attitude of the Sanusi towards the Turks and Enver Bey persuaded them to join with them and to take an oath to continue fighting as long as any Italians remained in Tripoli and Cyrenaica; indeed, they were the moving spirit in the resistance which the Italians had to meet, though even then they held aloof from a formal recognition of the Sultan's Khalifate: since the

Turkish evacuation the Sanusi considers himself as the sovereign ruler of Tripoli. For all this they were not disposed to act with the Turks against the British in the earlier part of the war; indeed, they seem to have been rather pre-disposed to assist the British, but the entrance of Italy into the war as one of the Allies made a material change and they then threw themselves into the conflict as supporters of Turkey. In the course of the war they made a campaign against the British in Egypt and gave considerable trouble, though more than once showing personal goodwill towards individual English, and they were not reduced until the autumn of 1916, when the British restrained them behind the Tripoli frontier, it being agreed that if they respected this boundary no effort would be made to follow them west of it. They remain still a problem for Italy to deal with in the future if she intends to carry out an effective occupation of Tripoli. The events of 1915-16 showed that the alarmist accounts of the formidable power of the Sanusi, which appear in works published before the war, and even in Prof. Macdonald's *Muslim Theology* (pp. 62-63) were greatly exaggerated. Like the Wahhabis under Ibn Saʻud, they were able to defy any external power attempting to invade their own country, safe in their remote position and protected by the miles of friendly desert through which an invader would have to pass, and are able to make rapid predatory excursions into any settled area on the desert edge for the very same reason which enabled the Arabs of the seventh century to attack Syria and Mesopotamia, because they are mobile in the desert, whilst armies unused to desert warfare cannot move there with ease and find it difficult to avail themselves of artillery; on the other hand the desert Arabs are especially exposed to air attack, and this will, no doubt, radically alter the conditions of future expeditions against desert tribes. The Sanusi in 1915-16 were largely armed with rifles taken from the Italians and by captured Russian rifles, which were brought across to Tripoli by submarine, and without some such supply of arms and ammunition by a helping western power, would not have been able to make the fight they did. But beyond the limitations which would have hindered the Sanusi in warfare with European forces is an internal and very serious source of weakness in the domestic rivalries by which the ruling dynasty is now divided and which undermine any permanent co-operation of the Sanusi tribes in military efforts. There are known to be disputes between the several sons of Muhammad ash-Sharif, the younger brother of Muhammad al-Mahdi, who died in 1896. The third son, Muhammad al-Abad (b. 1875), is on bad terms with his two elder brothers, the ruling Ahmad ash-Sharif and Muhammad Hallal, all sons by different mothers, because he, the third son, has seized the property of his maternal grandfather, 'Ali al-Ashab, at Tripoli: but it was chiefly the second son, Muhammad Hallal, a hot-headed young man (born 1893) who lent himself to Turkish and German intrigue. It would, however, be a mistake to suppose that their land can be conquered easily and they reduced to a subject position; they offer to Italy exactly the same problem that the Arabs of Mesopotamia offer to Great Britain; the permanent occupation and control of their territory can only be affected by an outlay of men and money which would be far in excess of any possible value to the conqueror. For a barren military glory such an occupation might be undertaken and even carried through, but it is certain that the home country would become extremely restive at the terrible cost and the great sacrifice of life involved. It would be a case of history repeating itself, of Hadria compelled by public opinion to retire from the land of the desert Arabs, whom Trajan had conquered at a heavy price, but whose continued control would have brought a vastly greater burden.

Very much on the same lines as the Wahhabis is the sect of the *Biyadhiyya*, which had its origin in 'Uman, and, apparently, has spread inland to South Arabia. According to Colonel Philby's account it dispenses with the *adhan*, or call to prayer, and with congregational prayer altogether (Philby: *In Desert Arabia*, ii. 228-9), but there does not seem to be much information available about its extent and present activity.

CHAPTER III

WESTERN PENETRATION OF ISLAM

THE world of Islam has been compelled to take serious notice of the progress, the peculiar tendencies, and the results of modern western civilization by reason of its extremely aggressive character. Only in Arabia have the Muslims been able to keep the west at arm's length, and even there this has been true only to a limited extent and bids fair soon to be a thing of the past: certainly 'Uman and Musqat have been brought into close contact with western life. In every other direction the lands of Islam have been permeated with western influences, some, such as Algeria, India, etc., are actually under western rule. It is difficult to classify and analyse the various forms which western influence has taken, and any such analysis must be more or less artificial, but we may perhaps venture to take political, economic, social, and intellectual effects as fairly indicating their main features.

The two earlier and more important cases of western interference were in India and Turkey. India, with a very considerable Muslim population, has become a part of the British Empire, and, since the virtual fall of the Mughuls in 1761, the English have been the practical rulers of this large body of Muslims. But it is a truism to say that India is a continent and not a country, and the Muslims form but a minority in face of a vast pagan population. Important by reason of their numbers, and including many of the most warlike and virile elements in the land, with moreover a tradition of empire, the Muslims of India form a very weighty factor in the world of Islam, although they are hardly in its centre in the same way as the Arabic speaking communities. British rule has been gradually extended over most of the Muslim peoples of India until now Afghanistan is the only one left beyond the pale. In India the penetration of Islam by western influences has been brought about directly by western rule, and, consequently, that penetration is more complete than in many lands nearer west.

The case of Turkey is different. Before western intervention several provinces, such as Algeria and Egypt, had become practically independent by the centrifugal tendency of a non-centralised control. Gradually these were seized by various western powers; first Algeria by France, who later on extended her sway over Tunis as well, Egypt and Syria by France also, but of these Egypt was not held and Syria retained only an international convention in the Lebanon, and later on Egypt, by reason of financial difficulties, fell into the hands of her European creditors, and the revolt of Arabi Pasha in 1882, resulted in British occupation, which became a protectorate in 1916, although throughout the promise was made that this would be only a temporary control. In 1912 the Italians seized the territory of Tripoli and they enforce their claim as against other European powers, though it does not appear that they are as yet able to render it effective.

Meanwhile Great Britain and Russia acting together practically partitioned Persia, and so in all directions it appeared that the western nations were deliberately partitioning the lands of Islam and exploiting them for their own advantage. It is true that no direct attack was made on Islam as a religion and all the European powers took the position that full religious freedom was to be maintained; but this did not quite carry conviction; the activities of Christian missionaries were protected and these had much more result than has been commonly supposed, especially in education. But apart from this there was a growing exploitation of Muslim countries for the material advantage of western financial interests, and Islam seemed to be rapidly passing into the position of an enslaved and subject community; even those countries which were not actually subjugated being put under the " sphere of influence " of some western power. Europeans had the impression that they could easily conquer any Muslim country at their own discretion, and took the same attitude in dealing with Asiatic countries which had a great history and the traditions of a military and ruling race as they took in dealing with the savage lands of

Africa. For a long time a strong feeling of dislike and fear had been growing in Asia towards the western powers and we must now endeavour to summarize the main causes of this feeling.

(1.) RELIGIOUS FEELING AGAINST EUROPEANS AS CHRISTIANS

In the first place must be put the feeling of Muslims against Europeans as Christians, not because it is the most potent factor in anti-European feeling but because it is one of the few reasons of dislike which can be definitely formulated and is the one most often assigned. Muslims, and more especially those who have never been in contact with Europeans, take the term " religion " in a sense rather different from that in which the word is commonly employed by us. It is not taken to denote simply a set of opinions on speculative theology, but implies a social order and group life of a definite kind : the Muslim eats, washes, and performs all the acts of daily life in a particular way, which differs from that of Christians, Jews, or heathen living in the same town and speaking the same language, though in fact it is by no means uncommon to find differences of dialect between Arabic speaking fellow-townsmen of different religions. Each religion in the East represents a social group with a more or less self-contained culture, and in many respects the term " religion " rather corresponds to what we understand by " nation " : indeed the Muslim is accustomed to regard Islam and Christendom as two " nations."

The mere political entity which we understand by the term, a very artificial application of the word and one of comparatively recent date, has no importance in the oriental mind, which is accustomed to group men according to religion and not according to political arrangements. The Muslim feels a certain brotherhood in Islam which binds together its adherents as against the non-Muslim world and imagines that Christendom is animated by a similar feeling of fraternity and loyalty. In the past such a feeling was recognised amongst Christians and survived down to the eighteenth century, when it was still felt as a disgraceful act of treachery for a Christian power to be allied with Muslims against another Christian state. It was only towards the end of that century and since, that more liberal thinkers in the West began to adopt the doctrine of the equality of men irrespective of their religion and culture, and to treat religion merely as a matter of private opinion. In Asia to-day the same attitude is in vogue which prevailed throughout Europe down to the latter part of the eighteenth century.

The average Muslim pictures all Christians as bound together by fraternal ties which produce a certain corporate spirit and lead to common action and mutual support, and this, it must be noted, is the attitude of the oriental Christian as well. In Egypt the writer has more than once been asked about the possible dangers to Muslims travelling in England, under the obvious impression that a Christian community would be likely to act in a hostile manner towards a non-Christian visitor, and the great grievance of the Copts is that the British authorities do not recognise their fellowship in Christianity by conceding them a favoured position. This does not imply that Muslims have any inclination to regard Christians as persons of peculiar piety, but simply that they take religion to denote a social grouping which causes its members to regard all outsiders as aliens.

Taking this attitude towards all religious groups and consequently towards Christendom, the Muslim is pre-disposed to attribute a considerable degree of fanaticism to Christians. In the near East the tradition of the Crusades is still alive and there is an inclination to suppose that the spirit which formerly led the whole group of Christian peoples to unite in a common attack upon Islam is still alive. Recent events have rather tended to endorse these ideas. The Balkan War of 1912-1913 proclaimed itself to be a crusade against Islam, and as such was largely acclaimed by the British Press: the Balkan races take the oriental standpoint in matters of religion. Moreover it has been the custom for the European powers to act as the official protectors of Christian communities, Russia as the champion of the Orthodox Greek Church, and France as that of the Latin Church, so much so, that very often Copts and Syrians, who suffered real or supposed harshness at the hands of Muslim rulers, joined the Uniat Churches, which are permitted to retain their own native liturgy, but are in communion with the Apostolic See, and by so doing come under the protection of the French consul. Although the educated Muslim is perfectly aware of the western principle of religious toleration, he very seldom appreciates the extent to which a real indifference as to religion has pervaded western politics.

Western influence also is responsible for the presence of Christian missionaries, and for the abrogation of the death penalty to which an apostate from Islam was formerly liable, both matters which may be explained by the principle of toleration, but which seem to indicate a pro-Christian attitude on the part of the western powers. It is extremely difficult to make anything like a fair estimate of the position of Christian missionary work in face of Islam. Obviously there are two main aspects to be considered : (i.) the attitude of the missionaries towards Islam which is naturally taken by the Muslim observer as indicating the real tendencies and aspirations of Christians ; and (ii.) the work actually accomplished. (i.) So far as the attitude of missionaries is concerned that is judged by their reported utterances, in private intercourse as well as in public, and by the literature which they circulate. It must be admitted that missionary literature of recent times differs very materially from that of a former generation. For the most part it is now free from the abusive and derisive tone and shows a more and less successful effort to understand and appreciate Islam ; the Prophet is no longer treated as an imposter, and very often there is evidence of an expert knowledge of Muslim theology and canon law. The purely rhetorical character of the older missionary tracts has not entirely disappeared but has passed very much into the background, and it is more generally recognised that it is the missionary's first duty to understand the religion with which he has to deal. In spite, however, of this change, missionary literature and missionary discourses must necessarily have a polemical character, and as this is the most accessible material for forming an opinion as to Christian teaching, it is inevitable that Muslims generally regard Christians as hostile. That this should be resented is somewhat unreasonable as Islam itself is a missionary religion and, as such, aggressive, and it seems more than probable that resentment is largely a phase of anti-European feeling. (ii.) As to the actual work of Christian missions, this must not be estimated by the number of converts, although there seems reason to believe that this is considerably more than is commonly supposed, but by the general influence exercised by mission schools, hospitals, etc. The schools do not exclude Muslim pupils, and in many cases they have won the confidence of Muslim parents who feel no reluctance to entrusting their children to them, but there are many who oppose them as propagandist. No doubt the mission schools do produce a certain number of converts as well as a large number of ex-pupils with a friendly attitude towards Christianity. At bottom it is a question of the personality of those engaged in teaching and the vast influence which a teacher with a convincing personality can exercise over his pupils ; the more obvious defect is that those in control are too anxious to introduce European social usages and customs which, though characteristically western are not necessarily Christian. But all this will be more properly considered as educational rather than religious. Although the actual results of missionary enterprise in Muslim lands are probably much more than is commonly supposed, there seems reason to believe that they are very small when compared with the effort made. Yet it would be altogether unreasonable to ignore their bearing upon the Muslim attitude towards Europe generally. Although the individual missionaries often win the friendship and esteem of Muslim neighbours to an exceptional degree, the very presence of missionary work must inevitably present Christianity in an aggressive light. The most outspoken opponents of missionary activity are usually the political and commercial Europeans in the community where that activity is in operation, and the motive of opposition is that the missionaries create difficulties by emphasizing religious differences which those others would prefer to have left in the background. This of itself proves that Christian missions are not negligible things : that they do provoke a certain measure of hostility amongst Muslims and thereby colour their view of Christian nations, and incline them to suppose that the crusading spirit is not extinct.

Yet the existence and work of Christian missions do not really form a crying grievance as Islam is well enough able to hold her own, and in Negro Africa where Christian and Muslim missionaries are in competition, it is estimated that ten heathen become Muslim for every one that becomes a Christian. The grievance only arises when Christian influence is, or seems to be, backed up by material force; it is the crusader who is feared, not the missionary. Rightly or wrongly, the impression has arisen that since 1914 the nations of Christendom have thrown off the mask and revealed themselves as inspired by a fanatical hatred of Islam and a determination to injure and humiliate it. Thus the Kwaja Kamal ud-Din says: " Unfortunately, the last thirty years have seen Islam being constantly weakened by the Christian Powers, and the Muslims in India have reason to suspect the presence of a British hand in this game against Islam. Prior to the war the process was one affecting the geographical boundaries of those countries, but the war itself could never have aroused such an upheaval of unrest in all Muslim lands, if the foolish policy of certain statesmen, egged on by religious bigotry in this country had not led Muslims to believe that the war was, after all, a war between Islam and Christianity." (Khwaja Kamal ud-Din: *India in the Balance*, Woking, 1922, pp. 52-53).

To us it may seem grotesque that a crusading spirit should be imputed to the governments of Western Europe, but from the Muslim point of view there is reasonable colour for suspecting an anti-Islamic animus. By 1914 the whole of Africa had been partitioned between the powers of Europe, with the exception only of Abyssinia and Liberia, and undoubtedly there was an intention to apply the same process to Asia. The true motive is greed, but those who were animated by this emotion were not unwilling to allow well-meaning but foolish persons to camouflage it under the specious pretext of bringing the blessings of civilization and Christianity to the East, and in the Near East there has been a disposition to acclaim every aggression in Muslim territories as a victory for Christianity; whilst the deliberate foundation of a Jewish state in Palestine, in territory already occupied and ruled by Muslims has produced a most unfavourable impression. Behind all this there is some reality, not in anything like the supposed anti-Muslim conspiracy, but a strong inclination to push Islam out of the way where it seemed to interfere with schemes of commercial aggression, and an attempt to manipulate the Muslim world by means of the Khalif. This has been based on the widespread but totally mistaken idea that the Khalif is a kind of Muslim Pope, and that the world of Islam can be controllde and worked through him in very much the same way that Ireland was controlled through the Vatican and the Episcopate. It became quite clear in 1922, when the Sultan Muhammad was forced to declare Mustapha Kemal a traitor, that he was no more than a tool in the hands of the Allied Powers occupying Constantinople, and the election of a new Khalif at Angora was a necessary expedient to preserve

Islam from the attempt to use the Khalif as a tool of the Western Powers, themselves more or less the tools of great international financial interests.

In general summary we may say that Muslims impute to Christian nations a crusading spirit which aims at the wrecking of Islam, and there are circumstances which appear to endorse this view, in reality so very wide of the mark. That the view is widespread, as undoubtedly is the case, shows that the Muslim world judges the motives of Christendom very inaccurately; an inaccuracy which has a close parallel in the common tendency of Christians to suppose that Islam is essentially fanatical.

(II.) THE FEELING AGAINST EUROPEANS AS IRRELIGIOUS

The tendency to regard Christians as fanatical and to suppose that Christendom is still animated by the spirit of the Crusades may be regarded as flourishing most amongst the less well informed and less observant Muslims, though by no means confined to them. Amongst many thoughtful Muslims objection to western influence is more truly made on the ground that it is rationalistic in tendency, that it undermines orthodox belief, and leads to the discarding of orthodox usages, and this objection is based on very real evidence in the irreligious attitude of those who have come under the influence of western education. It is not always perceived that in this respect Islam is not the only sufferer, for Christianity and Judaism are quite as definitely losing their hold on the younger generation, or survive only as a kind of humanitarianism more or less corresponding to Positivism. It is always a problem whether religion can keep pace with intellectual progress. In ancient Greece religion stood apart and the intellectual life of philosophy developed independently, but neither Christianity nor Islam would tolerate this divorce between the observances of religion and the intellectual life of the community, so that the question is whether religion can re-adjust itself to a new intellectual atmosphere. So far as Islam is concerned this is not the first time it has been faced by the problem; very early in its career the religion formed in an Arab atmosphere spread over lands already permeated with Hellenistic culture and it had to adapt itself to conditions not contemplated by its early professors. It did so adapt itself and formed its theology in the course of doing so, and thus it has in it a certain Hellenistic element which is capable of vigorous intellectual life. We shall later on consider the efforts which have been made to produce a liberal reform in Islam (cf. chap. IV. below): at present we are only concerned with the feeling that western thought is rationalistic in its tendency and so hostile to the orthodox faith of Islam, and for that reason that thought is repugnant to the devout Muslim.

(III) INFLUENCE OF WESTERN EDUCATION

One of the principal ideals of western liberalism in the nineteenth century was the application of western methods of education to Oriental lands; indeed education at home and abroad was then looked upon as a panacea, and the educational ideal lay in the direction of natural science and subjects of a more or less utilitarian value rather than in literary studies. Thus when western education was introduced into India and Egypt it was of the modern and commercial type and non-sympathetic towards classical standards. In such subjects as medicine and engineering modern tendencies were, of course, necessary and right, but in the material of a general education it was violently antagonistic to all the traditional standards of scholarship prevalent in the Muslim world, and in reality no less antagonistic to what is recognised as a classical education at home. Granted the difference that, since the Renascence, the western countries have taken the literature of ancient Greece and Rome as the basis of the "humanities," whilst the Muslim countries have taken Arabic literature, the general trend has been very much the same in both cases up to a point, at least if we take classical scholarship in the older sense of literature, grammar, and composition, such as was the case before the scientific study of archæology and comparative grammar was introduced. So far, then, as the humanities went the older education current in Islam had a strong resemblance to what was well established in the West, but the advocates of western education held aloof from this entirely, partly because the classical literature of Arabic very largely centres in the

Qur'an and so has a distinctly religious bearing which the Liberal, regarding religion as a purely private matter of individual opinion, had no desire to touch, and the Muslim, from reasons of an entirely different character, was not willing to allow him to touch, and partly because the typical Liberal of the nineteenth century strongly inclined to scientific in preference to literary subjects. Thus the western education introduced to the Orient was of a character entirely out of touch with the traditional standards, and, to a large extent, it has not been recognised as education. The average Muslim regards western scientific education simply as a species of craftsmanship, a knowledge extremely useful for certain purposes and especially so for the pursuit of wealth and ambition, but in no sense connected with learning or scholarship, which are to be found in the mosque and not in the English or American school. The youth who, after making progress in the European school, cuts himself loose and reverts to the traditional system of the mosque, is respected as one who has sacrificed a promising and lucrative trade for the pursuit of learning. European education is in a sense admired, but it is certainly not respected.

In the mid-nineteenth century the western world assumed that its educational methods were perfect and efficient in all respects, that they were bound to raise all those to whom they were applied, and that there was no alternative worthy of serious consideration, and so they were applied in India and Egypt with all their western details of examinations, etc., without the slightest doubt as to their efficacy. But education did not cease to develop in the West and the educationalist of to-day is by no means so sure that the methods in vogue in the middle years of the nineteenth century were so satisfactory as was then supposed; or rather, we may say, that the general consensus of educationalists is that they were very unsatisfactory, though the experts differ amongst themselves as to the remedy, not from lack of choice, for the course of education for the last seventy years is strewn with the débris of discarded systems, each acclaimed in its own day as a heaven-sent solution, and each passing into contempt as it was superceded by another. To-day it is recognised that there are problems in education, experiments of various kinds are being tried and are watched sympathetically, but probably the only point on which educationalists are unanimous is in repudiating the pert assurance of the extremely mechanical methods which were exalted as the perfection of education by the progressives of sixty years ago. Those methods, which regarded the very cream of educational efficiency as the severity of an examination test, were to the front when English schools were established in India and Egypt, and thus the methods now admitted to be defective in this country are still held up as the ideal standards in those schools, and it must be noted that some of the defects commonly charged against the westernized native are very much the same which have been recognised as defects in our own education and have been the cause of changes being made here, such, for example, as lack of co-relation in knowledge, in scrappy and superficial teaching, in excessive regard for the display to be made at an examination, in knowledge of details without grasp of the underlying principle and similar matters. It is not true to say that western education has produced the *babu* type, for the civil administration of native governments in former times also produced its clerk type with peculiarities more or less offensive to those who had to do business with officials. Western education certainly has given a new kind of peculiarity which is peculiarly offensive to the old-fashioned Muslim, but the more serious result is that it has produced the clerk class in too great a quantity by the introduction of state supported education and has thus manufactured an educated proletariat which, as always is the case, is ripe for very seditious movement and sore with grievance against those who have prompted their education, and then either failed to provide them with employment or provided it with inadequate remuneration. In India and Egypt the main strength of agitation lies in the subordinate employés of the State and in the disappointed competitors for employment, and in this connection it is important to remember that western education is looked upon solely as a form of craftsmanship to be followed as a livelihood and not as a branch of culture for the development of the intellectual life, a view which the Muslim takes only of the traditional literary education given in the mosque. To the Muslim, therefore, western influence appears as hostile to culture and as tending to sacrifice scholarship for commercial success.

It is necessary here to mention a certain measure of reaction on the part of some Liberal Muslims who exert themselves to claim that all really of value in western science is ultimately derived from the East. In this, of course, there is a measure of truth as the mediæval West received a great part —though not all—of its knowledge of Greek philosophy and science through the medium of Arabic writers, who not only transmitted but also continued the development of its content. Unfortunately the writers who are most vigorous in maintaining this thesis tend to over-state their case ; though indeed not much would be served by its proof.

(iv) Western Influence as Producing Social Changes

Islam is not simply a creed, it is a social order, and that order is very seriously affected by contact with a social order of a totally different type developed in the West, though not in all cases for the worst. The main features of this change may be summarised as follows :—

(a) *Marriage and Divorce.*

It is now generally held that there have been two leading stages in the evolution of marriage as it exists in civilized communities, ignoring for the present certain more primitive phases which do not apply to our present argument. In the earlier of these two, the *mot'a* marriage, the man is a temporary visitor of the woman who retains her position in her own tribe; her children are reckoned as belonging to that tribe, and she is liable to terminate the connection at her discretion. The later, or *ba'al* marriage, shows a union in which the wife is captured or purchased and becomes the property of the husband, her children belong to him, and she can be disposed of like any other property. These two forms result in social conditions which are known respectively as *matriarchal* and *patriarchal*. This view is based on the investigations of the brothers McLennan some fifty years ago, and, although later research may perhaps modify some of the details of their theories, this general relationship of the *mot'a* and *ba'al* marriages seems to hold good. In the time of the Prophet the Arabs of Arabia had advanced beyond the stage of *mot'a* marriages and accepted those of the *ba'al* type, but this change was then a recent one, so that the woman of the *mot'a* union had not yet sunk to the position of a harlot, although that kind of union had ceased to be respectable. Aghani (xvi. 106) refers to it as a well known custom of the *Jahiliya* or " time of ignorance," but disapproves of it as " the sister of harlotry." Such temporary marriage is still recognised by Shi'ite law, and the Roman historian Ammianus Marcellinus, some two centuries before Muhammad, refers to it as then the normal type of Arab marriage (Amm. Marc. xiv. 4). Now it is extremely important for us to remember when dealing with the subject of Muslim marriages, the surprisingly early stage of development which the Arabs had reached at the time of the Prophet's ministry; indeed, they seem hardly to have advanced from primitive barbarism when we compare them with the population of the Roman Empire, and it may well be that a very great uplift was made by the Prophet, and yet the Arabs were in a backward condition, for all progress is relative. In Madina, the Prophet was in contact with Jewish law and influenced by this he raised the prevalent type of *ba'al* marriage to a much more stable condition and a higher level than had been known in pre-Islamic Arabia; the number of lawful wives was limited to four (Qur. 4, 3) and to them fairly ample rights were secured. It became a man's duty to provide for them, they had a right to inheritance, their property remained at their own disposal and was not merged in that of their husbands, and divorce needed a formal repudiation pronounced before witnesses (cf. Qur. 4, passim). All this may seem to us very far short of securing for wives the position which they ought to occupy in civilized society, but we must contrast it with the position of the pre-Islamic wife in a *ba'al* marriage, where the woman was simply the possession and like any other captive without rights. The *ba'al* marriage probably began with the taking of female captives for wives, and as captives they were no more than slaves, the preference for this kind of marriage being largely due to the fact that it put the husband in the position of master instead of being merely a suitor as in the earlier *mot'a* union, so that the tendency was to emphasize the mastership very strongly and, in the ordinary course, many centuries would have to pass before any disposition arose to modify this mastership by admitting a wife's rights even in a very moderate degree ; but Muhammad, in contact with a much more advanced social culture, made a leap over centuries of evolution and set the Muslim standard of marriage far in advance of what had been prevalent in pre-Islamic times, even though the level reached fell far short of what had been attained in the Roman Empire. It is nonsense to talk of Muhammad pandering to the sensuality of his adherents by allowing a low morality : the standard he set was a relatively high one. Unfortunately every reform has in it the danger that it may be established permanently and so act as a barrier against further progress, and this has been the case especially in Islam, where the great prestige of the Prophet has caused the work of reform in so many respects to stop short where he left it.

In the Roman Empire social development had reached a very much more advanced level, and Christianity developed in surroundings in which monogamy was becoming the normal standard, though this was seriously injured by the facility of divorce. In the divorce question the Christian Church early took a very definite position regarding marriage as a very permanent union, or at least only to be dissolved by adultery, which was the view of the Eastern Church, and then, at a slightly later period, adultery was extended so as to cover fornication by a married man as well as that involving a married woman. When Christianity reached the position that irregular intercourse on the husband's part was adulterous that is to say, when it was taught that the husband must be faithful as well as the wife, then indirectly Christianity was committed to strict monogamy, although in fact the New Testament has recorded no command which restricts a man to one wife but only expresses a preference for " the husband of one wife " in the case of a person appointed to the office of bishop (I. Tim. iii., 1—2). We do not maintain that polygamy ever was actually tolerated in the Christian Church, but merely point out that in the evolutionary progress of society a permanent union with fairly equal rights to either party, which involves monogamy, is in the nature of things a late development which was reached by the Christian Church in the atmosphere of Roman society where circumstances were ripe for this development, but Arabian society, though tending in that direction, was many centuries behind. Properly we may surmise that monogamy and permanence of marriage would have been attained gradually in the normal course of evolution, but the Prophet's precedent tended to crystallize the stage reached in the seventh century and so retarded evolution. There is nothing in Islam which directly insists on plurality of wives or acts as an incentive to divorce ; it is merely that the law permits and contents itself with placing some restrictions on the absolute freedom which the husband enjoyed in pre-Islamic times. Under western influence a tendency has arisen to prefer monogamy and to feel that divorce needs some reasonable excuse, some grounds other than mere caprice. It is striking to note the frequency with which these topics are treated in the dramatic productions of the younger Egyptian playwrights : very often the drama turns on the harsh treatment of a wife who is supplanted by a rival or is discarded, and in these plays, crude efforts as they often are, the moral standard is that theoretically assumed in the West. To this the more rigid Muslim finds no objection : he would oppose, indeed, a law forbidding polygamy or altering the conditions of divorce as infringing on the canon law, but the growth of a feeling in these directions has nothing inconsistent with Muslim teaching : though the western custom of investigating matrimonial difficulties in open court strongly offends Muslim ideas of decency.

Here it is inevitable that we should touch upon the relations of the sexes generally. The modern tendency in western life is towards sex equality, and this certainly is not acceptable to Islam. In practice and in law the Muslim wife has rights over property which the married woman in England did not enjoy until quite recent times, but Muslim countries generally are at a stage of social evolution when the safe-guarding of the woman is too urgent to allow her independent activity : perhaps the *mot'a* marriage is still near enough to cast a tone of indecency upon the independence of women.

The external standards of morality are amongst the most artificial and capricious conventions of civilized society, and it is not easy for the western mind to appreciate those which prevail in Muslim society. The custom has arisen, not primitive and not universal, but widely prevalent, of requiring women to be secluded and veiled from the gaze of strange men. From this has arisen a standard of propriety entirely different from anything with which we are familiar, a standard which results in an extreme prudery in particular directions. Assuming that a sound morality must be based on quite natural and healthy conditions it follows that every form of prudery, which is the artificial dissimulation of natural relations, tends to produce abnormal and unhealthy results. Women are veiled and segregated, and decency requires their existence to be more or less ignored, an obviously unreal and artificial state of affairs. It is a grave impropriety to enquire after the female members of a family; it is an offence against decency to allow women to perform on the stage, and so female parts are taken by boys, or sometimes by foreign women, towards whom no respect is observed, and even amatory poetry must conventionally represent the loved one as a male. To us the result is as offensive as our condition of allowing free intercourse between sexes is to a Muslim. Both Christian and Muslim, it must be admitted, are very far from anything like an ideal morality, but Islam comes out the worse from the comparison, not as the result of greater laxity, but by reason of a more artificial prudery. The veiling and seclusion of women deprives the male of that natural companionship and intercourse with the opposite sex, which to many is a psychological necessity during the approach of maturity, and tends even to make the wife unfit for companionship. Sex, it appears, craves not only carnal intercourse but the type of companionship which may be termed the romantic friendship, and the oriental conditions prevent either the wife or the harlot from satisfying, for the woman of loose life in oriental communities does not correspond to the *hetaira* of ancient Greece. These conditions produce an abnormal and artificial state ; the young man grows up in an exclusively male society from which women are secluded as companions, and in such a state there arises a tendency to form relations which are at base romantic friendships with persons of the male sex. We are accustomed to regard such relations as abnormal and immoral, but in fact they are generally due to perfectly normal and natural impulses operating in an abnormal and unnatural atmosphere : the love which would, under other conditions, seek its object in the opposite sex, is checked and seeks an outlet in a different direction, and so a particular form of vice, unfortunately helped by literary conventions, becomes unusually prevalent. No doubt this is not an adequate or complete explanation of the whole psychology of the matter, for this has never been very completely treated, but it does seem safe to say that the restrictions produced by abnormal conditions which prevent intercourse and companionship between the sexes are bound to result in tendencies which are not so much abnormal as abnormally directed. It is curious to note that in every country the introduction of what is termed unnatural vice is described as of late date and due to foreign influence, usually to that of aliens who are politically obnoxious. To this Islam is no exception, and one would gather from the Arabic historians that the austere morals of the early Arabs were corrupted by Persian captives in the days of the first few Khalifs. Probably there is some measure of truth in this, as it seems likely that the singers and slaves imported from conquered Persia introduced luxurious and vicious habits to an extent unknown to the hardy and frugal Arabs of a more primitive age. It was one of the penalties of civilization, and very likely the professional class of *khawal* (pl. *khuwal*) now existing in some, but not in all Muslim countries, had its origin in those times. Aghani and other historians relate how the authorities of Mecca and Madina took severe measures against persons of this class. It cannot be too clearly emphasized that the worst elements on the moral side in Islam are due, not to a desire to pander to lascivious tastes, but to a pronounced but wholly mistaken prudery which has throughout history given a strongly puritan and persecuting tone to official orthodox Islam.

We may say, indeed, that some of the most

urgent dangers resulting from the contact of East and West arise, not from a conflict between higher and lower moral standards, but from the conflict of two moral standards which have developed on somewhat divergent lines. Western ideas have undermined Muslim standards, and all moral standards are easily undermined by reason of their extremely artificial and illogical character, but have not succeeded in putting new standards in their place, so that the result has been an increased moral laxity, and very often an attitude towards women on the part of those who have received a western education which is indecent in the eyes of older Muslims. The circulation of the inferior type of French novel, describing social conditions very different from those assumed in the Muslim world and totally misunderstood by the readers, familiarity with the variety entertainments promoted by the less desirable class of Levantines, and a misconstruction of the liberty allowed to western women, have all produced a tendency amongst young men of the progressive type to discard conventional restrictions, superficial as they admittedly were, hitherto maintained towards women of honourable character, and thus western influence seems to cause a relaxation of morals and a corruption of youth.

(b) The Family₁

If we are correct in diagnosing the difference between western and Islamic ideas about matrimony as being at base a difference in the stage of development reached and, in the case of Islam, of a check of evolution at that particular stage, we are on surer ground in treating the family on similar lines. Muslim society postulates the solidarity of the family unit and this implies the case in Western Europe also, but it is at present passing away though it is by no means so much a thing of the past as to need to be illustrated by antiquarian research. The novelist Balzac more than once deplores the change as one taking place in his own day in France, and in the Latin countries both law and custom still imply a measure of family solidarity : it is only the Bolshevik who, as yet, declares for the abolition of the family altogether. But undoubtedly the modern trend of western opinion has greatly relaxed the ties which formerly bound the members of a family together, and the introduction of western ideas has produced a similar tendency in Young Islam. Consequently western influence is denounced as undermining the obedience due to the head of the family and as tending to substitute a selfish individualism for the traditional solidarity ; all, in fact, an echo of what Balzac has already denounced about the tendencies of revolutionary France.

In this and such like matters the important things are not the great ones but rather the small ones. It is not a question of domestic rebellion and open revolt, but of a new attitude towards life and its duties, an attitude which is offensive because it cuts loose from accepted standards and the conventions of traditional sanction, and this is the more effective in arousing repugnance because it is an offence against the *mores*, that is to say, against the usual standards of the social order in which we live.

(c) *Democracy.*

To-day the western world is accustomed to declare that democracy represents the perfect ideal of human society. The term itself is somewhat comprehensive, not to say vague, in its application, but at bottom it represents the egalitarian principles which are a heritage from the French revolution and which imply the equality of all men irrespective of colour, religion, or race. In practice it generally works out as the rule of the majority, on the theory that, if all are equal, a numerical majority necessarily implies a superiority before which the minority must give way. Writers very often refer to early Islam as even more democratic than modern Europe, but in this application democracy has rather a different meaning : it does not imply the equality of men, but only the equality of Muslims. In that sense Islam is, if we may so express it, a democratic caste, a kind of freemasonry whose members are, at least in theory, equal as amongst themselves, but with a class-barrier which separates them from an immeasurably inferior non-Muslim world. It is not difficult to find passages which emphasize the equality of all who trace their common descent to Adam, but these are always in context of reproof to those who claimed family honours. Islam has never recognized a real fraternity between Muslim and non-Muslim, and the attempt to break down the privileged position of the faithful means undermining an orthodox article of belief. Such an attempt actually does appear in certain Sufi quarters where it was held that the traditional forms of religion are only means of leading men to the one reality which is God, but in this, just as in the substitution of perpetual intercourse with God for the stated liturgical prayers, Sufism is at variance with orthodox Islam, and it must be remembered that this divergent tendency towards mysticism is a centrifugal force which has long been straining the tension of orthodox Muslim teaching. Thus the great Persian mystic Abu Sa'id ibn Abi l-Khayr says:—

"Not until every mosque beneath the sun
Lies ruined, will our holy work be done;
And never will true Musalman appear
Till faith and infidelity are one."

(Nicholson: *Mystics of Islam*, Lond. 1914, p. 90). But this is an extreme form of Sufi teaching and exceptional: for the most part the Sufis remain loyal to the tradition of orthodox Islam, although behind them is a spirit tending towards a mysticism which strives to break loose from Muslim restrictions. It is this Sufi spirit which is most effective in the actual spiritual life of present day Islam, and the tendency to evolve a simple monotheism in which every worshipper of the One God is recognized as a true believer must not be overlooked.

At present, in Arabia, the modified Sufism of al-Ghazali as developed by the Sayyid Murtada (d. 1790 A.D.) is the great revival of the theology of Ibn Taymiya, the doctor of the Wahhabis, and represents the predominant school of Mecca and the Hijaz. In the opinion of Professor Macdonald (*Muslim Theology*, p. 285) " these two tendencies then—that back to the simple monotheism of Muhammad and that to an agnostic mysticism—are the hopeful signs of modern Islam." We shall refer later (cf. pp. 111-119 below) to the Babist movement, of Muslim origin though disclaimed by orthodox Islam, which takes very much the same extreme position as Abu Sa'id, and it is this movement, it must be noted, which has surpassed the rest of Islam in gaining adherents in England and America.

For our present purpose, however, we perceive that the theory of democracy which tends to teach the equality of Muslims and non-Muslims, is repugnant to orthodox Islam, and is regarded as one of the western influences which are detrimental to religion.

(*d*) *Courtesy.*

Throughout the East a great deal of importance is attached to the punctilious observance of outward and conventional formalities which are taken as characteristic of the intercourse to be observed between civilized persons. These formalities are extremely artificial, and those observed amongst Muslims differ considerably from those prevalent amongst Hindus, Chinese, etc., but in each community or religion they form an external politeness which has strong traditional and religious endorsement, and represents all that would be regarded as good form in western opinion. Modern tendencies in the West incline strongly to discard the more formal usages of courtesy and this has become strongly marked in the twentieth century; a brusque tone has arisen, an impatience with traditional formalities as inconsistent with the business requirements of the age, and a disposition to ignore what our fathers called " politeness " because they, like the Orientals, identified these observances with culture. If the brusquerie of modern intercourse is at variance with the conventional usages of a generation not long past, it is still more in opposition to the older fashioned and still more exacting formalities of Oriental culture. The Muslim who has been much in contact with Westerns is able to recognize that western attitude is natural, and very often he inclines to discard his own conventions and to regard this as a mark of progress, but to many the attitude and manner of the western, and more particularly of the commercial, who is impatient of the waste of time involved in the elaborate formalities of oriental intercourse, are directly offensive. And this holds good, not only on the negative side by non-observance of expected courtesies very largely expressed in set sentences to be used on specified occasions—a proper salutation and a proper reply at almost every minor incident of ordinary intercourse—but very frequently the western adopts a tone of rough jocularity and "chaff" which is entirely foreign to oriental usage and is regarded as extremely offensive, the more so as the western generally expects a measure of deference and respect from the oriental, and himself resents the liberties he so freely takes. Occasionally one may see a native actor reproduce in mimicry the mannerisms of the westerner as they strike the oriental mind— the brusquerie, the sudden fits of uncontrolled temper, and the unrestrained laughter, but it is not always easy for a western observer to see reproductions of this kind. No doubt the caricature, however exaggerated, conveys a fairly true idea of the general impression from the oriental point of view, and if so the western appears as a rough and boorish person, choleric and impatient, entirely devoid of the courtesies which are the traditional small change of social intercourse. Now it must be admitted that impressions of this kind are not trivial things: they colour very strongly the relations between different nations and have more than once in the past contributed appreciably to international animosities. An acute observer, Meredith Townsend, some twenty years ago wrote: "It is very difficult, of course, for an Englishman, conscious of his own rectitude of purpose and benevolence of feeling, to believe that he will not be more liked when he is better known; but a good many facts seem to show that it is not so. He is not seen and talked to anywhere by men of a different race so much as he is in Ireland, and he is not hated quite so much anywhere else. He is decidedly much more disliked in Egypt since he appeared there in such numbers. He is more hated in the sea-coast towns of India, where he is prominent, busy, and constantly talked to, than he is in the interior where he is rarely seen ; much more detested in the planter districts than in the districts where he is only a rare visitor. If there is contempt for him anywhere in India, it is in the great towns, not in the rural stations, where he is so nearly invisible ; and contempt is of all forms of race-hatred the most dangerous." (Meredith Townsend : *Asia and Europe,* 2nd Ed. Lond. 1903 p. 216). These words apply not only to India but to every case where social groups of different type are in close contact and express not a race-hatred strictly so called, not a national or religious or cultural animosity, though all these may contribute, but simply a class-feeling, which is particularly pronounced as between the ruling and subject communities ; it may slumber and be buried when the two types are not in close contact, but contact generally tends to " get upon the nerves " of one or both. There can be no question that now, as in the Indian Mutiny of 1857, the prime motive of all the anti-British agitation is personal dislike of the English as a body, and the chief movers in such agitation are invariably those who have been most in contact with them ; very often those who have received a western education.

(v.) Economic Causes

Asiatic society generally rests upon an agricultural basis, the craftsmen forming only a small minority and not usually enjoying great esteem. To a large extent this was the case in Europe also until the nineteenth century, when industrialism began to develop on a large scale and totally changed the economic structure of society. The peasant, who had definite rights which he inherited from a long past which went ultimately back to tribal conditions, and which was not barely economic in its character, at least in the older civilizations in Europe, was gradually replaced by the wage-earner, whose undefined position led to a fierce struggle between him and his employer; a struggle which to a large extent is still in progress and its issue uncertain. On the side of the wage-earner the struggle became more and more difficult by the increase of scale in the organization of factories until the workers lost much of their individuality and became merely units in a vast machine, and as the controllers of this machine ceased themselve to be individuals with a human interest in their employés, and became corporate bodies, the conditions of the worker's life became more and more grim and forbidding. On the side of the employer the use of capital was developed to a degree unprecedented in history; great corporations were able to buy out or crush other employers, and finally a capitalist class developed behind the actual employers and was able to manipulate them as well as the workers and to become formidable rivals of the political governments. This capitalist class owed its power to its financial resources, not necessarily to the money it owned, but largely to the money it could control ; very often it took no real interest in the industry it financed, and of which it was profoundly ignorant, and it was often under the control of an alien race, whose interests were not identical with those either of the workers or of the employers, and exploited both these classes mercilessly. In the early years of the twentieth century these conditions assumed more formidable proportions ; practically every one of the western governments was more or less the tool of groups of international financiers who reaped the real benefit of the work done and did not pretend the least consideration for those in their employ, to whom they were total strangers. A new social order had arisen in which not only the actual labourer but even the skilled manager was pitilessly exploited, not deliberately, for in many cases efforts were made to secure humane conditions, but by the very force of circumstances, by the segregation of the classes, and by the very vastness and complicated character of the machine evolved. It is true that there were benefits in which the workers shared, material prosperity and improved conditions of life which affected all classes of the community, but against this modern western civilization had developed a cruel tone and obviously the real ones to benefit were those of the capitalist class strictly so called ; the group of international financial exploiters. Never before in human history had the power of capital developed to such proportions, and the wonderful results achieved in the West caused those capitalists to turn covetous glances to the comparatively undeveloped resources of Africa and Asia. Pressure was brought to bear upon European governments, and they, manipulated by powerful financial corporations, were compelled to interfere in other lands in order to obtain concessions, and employed the resources of the home country and the lives of its citizens to protect commercial enterprises and assure good profits for the investors: very much of the imperialism of the later nineteenth and the twentieth centuries was not due to the aspirations and ambitions of the citizens of the great western powers, but to the pressure of wealthy corporations who were glad to manipulate imperialistic ambitions for their own advantage, and were the ones really benefited thereby. By 1914 all Africa, with the exception of Abyssinia, which had been able to resist the Italians successfully, and Liberia, which enjoyed a guarantee from the United States, had been partitioned amongst the western powers, and the scramble for Asia was beginning to follow that for Africa.

The introduction of these grim and forbidding features of western life into the East and the obvious determination to exploit Asia in the same way as Africa was bound to arouse resentment and resistance amongst those who found their traditional existence encroached upon by a new condition of industrial servitude, a condition for which increased material advantages was not felt to be adequate compensation, the less so because it was accompanied by a steadily increased cost of living. Although the factory hands in India receive wages which are absurdly small compared with those paid in England, France, or America, they really are dear labour for they have never been able to settle to these new industrial conditions, which are intensely repugnant to them, and industry can only command the services of an inferior class : in fact, the poorer Asiatic is still a peasant at heart, and it is only the actual failures and bad men of the villages who are willing to be drawn in to the industrial machine, or else those who for a comparatively high wage are willing to work in it for a time, but cut themselves loose as soon as they have enough to invest in agriculture.

These feelings are best expressed in the words which the Bolshevik *Izvestia* puts in the mouth of the Afghan envoy to Moscow: " I am neither Communist nor Socialist, but my political programme so far is the expursion of the English from Asia. I am an irreconcilable enemy of European capitalism in Asia, the chief representative of which are the English. On this point I coincide with the Communists, and in this respect we are your natural allies." (cited, Stoddard : *New World of Islam*, p. 287). Islam dreads the new and sinister form assumed by the civilization of Western Europe, which has replaced the humanitarian attitude of the nineteenth century, and shows a return to the relentless exploitation which characterized the policy of the East India Company in the eighteenth century. Present conditions are very different from those of the nineteenth century, when in

1848 Lord Palmerston circularised the British representatives in foreign states to the effect that, " It has hitherto been thought by the successive governments of Great Britain undesirable that British subjects should invest their capital in loans to foreign governments instead of employing it in profitable undertakings at home," a statement which has even stronger application to commercial undertakings in lands not under British rule which have come to the fore-front since 1848. It is no longer a question of the British Government's discretion of invention to secure the due performance of commercial contracts; the State itself is little more than the tool of the powerful corporations which employ the nation's prestige, the taxpayer's money, and the citizens' lives to secure their dividends.

(VI.) THE RACE AND COLOUR QUESTION

This is one of the most perplexing and curious phases of group psychology and one which has not yet received anything like adequate treatment at the hands of psychologists. Racial antipathies undoubtedly do exist and presumably are produced by definite causes and governed by laws, but these are as yet quite obscure. We find no evidence of any such antipathy to those of a different colour before the seventeenth century, and it then begins to appear only very occasionally and generally mixed with religious and political prejudices. Its later development has been capricious in the extreme; it appears strongly marked in the Spanish and Portuguese settlers in South America, but is absent from the Portuguese in the East Indies ; it is acute amongst the Dutch colonists in South Africa, but does not prevail amongst the Dutch in the Indies. It shows itself in an attitude of conscious superiority which may develop into a kindly patronage, the " bearing of the white man's burden " and attempting to educate the subject people according to the ideas of the ruling race, or it may develop into a caste exclusiveness which treats the subject population as an inferior race which must not be permitted any freedom of intercourse with the superior caste. It is, of course, quite easy to pass from the former phase to the latter, and this is by no means infrequent when the European, conscious of his own kindly intentions and confident in the superiority of his culture, considers that his beneficence has been met with ingratitude. It is very common to find that the attitude of aloofness is regarded as peculiarly an attribute of the English, overlooking the fact that the number of English in contact with Orientals is far in excess of that of any other of the western nations, and that, whilst there are very many stiff English, there are very many also who are singularly happy in their intercourse with Oriental peoples : one may venture upon the opinion that, on the average, the English are at least as fortunate as the French and Italians, who allow a greater familiarity but turn upon natives rather sharply at any liberty and then show a degree of imperiousness and even arrogance which

Englishmen rarely display. At the same time it must be remembered that many orientals are extraordinarily thin-skinned and unduly sensitive to any fancied slight, and this is perhaps particularly so with Egyptians, as though indeed it were a kind of hysteria, possibly the penalty of too long a period of civilization. However this may be, the fact remains that racial antipathy does exist, though one of the most difficult things to diagnose or explain; it is felt on both sides, but naturally takes it acutest form amongst those who feel themselves treated as the inferior race. The Muslims of Asia, Egypt, and North Africa are not savage or semi-savage people like the negroes of Africa; they have the traditions of a military and of a ruling community, and cannot be regarded from the same point of view as the black people.

Undoubtedly the expression of European ideas of superiority has become more pronounced and more arrogant in recent times, or else the opportunities of contact have been more frequent, or the subject communities have found the tolerance of British rule more favourable for the unrestrained expression of resentment.

(VII.) POLITICAL OBJECTIONS

In the very nature of things the subject community resents the position of the ruling class, and the wider apart these are by race, religion, and general culture, the more sorely is this resentment felt. Unfortunately the history of the last fifty years contains grounds for accentuating this feeling.

In the nineteenth century the western nations were influenced by Liberal principles of a strongly humanitarian character : that the profession of these was often extremely hypocritical may be true, but every nation which had to deal with oriental races made such profession, and it more or less restrained its policy towards those over whom it had control. In the sixteenth century the Spaniards and Portuguese adopted a policy of frank exploitation by conquest, and in the New World pressed this to its logical conclusions ; by a Papal grant these two powers had the newly-discovered lands divided between them and proceeded to take possession and to subdue their inhabitants. In this conquest the other nations of Europe did not take part, not by reason of any humanitarian scruples, but simply because they were not strong enough to dispute the Spanish-Portuguese monopoly. Towards the end of the century the English began to share and, so far as America was concerned, acted simply as pirates until they managed to secure a field for their own exploitation. Later on, it is true, the English, Dutch, and French adventurers who began operations in Africa and the East recognized the rights of native sovereigns and made bargains with them, but this only in so far as they were unable to carry out open conquest. When a series of unforeseen circumstances placed the English in control of the Empire of the Mughul Kings of Delhi they began a period of tyranny and exploitation of exceptional unscrupulousness : but this was due to greed rather than to wanton cruelty, and the conduct of Burke in the trial of Warren Hastings aroused and formulated a definite conscience in this country and abroad in relation to the responsibility incurred by a European power ruling over oriental subjects. From the time of Burke onward this conscience was maintained and produced a definitely humanitarian attitude which assumed that the " white man " must rule for the benefit of his oriental subjects, that he ought to impose his own civilization upon them, by force if necessary, but always for their ultimate benefit, it being assumed as self-evident that western civilization was immeasurably superior and that it was only a kind of culpable ignorance which prevented the oriental from seeing this. It was taken for granted that when orientals once saw the blessings of civilization as they flourished in the West they would become their ardent advocates and, with this end in view, Indians, Egyptians, and others, were brought to England and France and then, to the humanitarian's astonishment, they very often concluded that the civilization they saw in the West was of a kind they did not want to see at home at all. But with the twentieth century a change, subtle but very decided, came over all this. Humanitarian professions were made as freely as ever, but it gradually became clear that the spirit behind was altered : the attempt to veil greed and rapacity was more perfunctory, and the older tradition of exploitation began to show through the disguise. The scramble for Africa showed the change, and a similar scramble for Asia was clearly foreshadowed.

The altered conditions were most plainly seen in the striking contrast between China and Japan in the Far East. In the nineteenth century Japan turned a friendly ear to the missionaries of western civilization and Europe looked on with kindly encouragement as it began to copy the conditions and reputed blessings of the West. For a while the Japanese wondered whether they ought to include the Christian religion, but shrewdly perceived that the nations of the West were no longer very deeply attached to Christianity and did not expect this but only desired to see religious toleration. After a little further hesitation the Japanese decided to develop Shinto as their national religion, though expressing willingness to tolerate any other. All this was viewed with benevolent encouragement and indulgence : apparently the West was delighted to welcome a new recruit to its culture. In the twentieth century China in like manner developed a determination to adopt western civilization, but had a very different experience. The change only precipitated the seizure of China and its partition between the rival powers who were no longer benevolent sponsors blessing the birth of a new nation in western form but rather a gathering of brigands restrained only by their own rivalries as to the sharing of the spoil.

A new atmosphere arose mainly from the causes upon which we have already touched. Behind the political governments were now great financial interests, very often international in their character, and these took the attitude which Macaulay describes as that of the East India Company in the eighteenth century, " The Directors, it is true, never enjoined or applauded any crime. Far from it. Whoever examines their letters written at that time will find there many just and humane sentiments, many excellent precepts, in short, an admirable code of political ethics. But every exhortation is modified or nullified by a demand for money. ' Govern leniently, and send more money ; practise strict justice and moderation towards neighbouring powers, and send more money,' this is, in truth, the sum of all the instructions that Hastings ever received from home. Now these instructions, being interpreted mean simlpy, ' Be the father and the oppressor of the people ; be just and unjust, moderate and rapacious.' " And this always must be the tendency when government is in the hands of a trading corporation, whether a chartered company administering an area, or a financial trust operating as the power behind the throne.

CHAPTER IV

REACTION OF ISLAM AGAINST THE WEST

WE have just enumerated some of the reasons which may have helped in preventing the western nations and their particular form of civilization form appealing to the oriental peoples. But, it must be admitted, there are many to whom they have appealed and amongst them are Muslims who have been profoundly influenced by western thought, not to the extent of abandoning their own religion and culture, but in re-formulating these under the influence of the West. As we have elsewhere noted this had a close precedent in the results of the penetration of Islam by Hellenistic thought in the course of the eighth and ninth centuries and has a modern parallel in the way in which Christianity has been, and is being, modified under the influence of the progress of modern thought.

It is, naturally, in India where the contact of Islam with western education has been closest, that we see the clearest evidences of what may be described as a Liberal movement in Islam. This is especially associated with *Sir Sayyid Ahmed Khan*, of Delhi, who founded the " British Indian

Association" in 1866. He was primarily an educationalist, and as such a whole-hearted advocate of western education, and his efforts resulted in the establishment of a Muslim College at Aligarh where pupils received a thoroughly modern English education, but are, at the same time, trained on definitely Muslim lines so far as relates to religious teaching. Although he desired the pupils at this college to remain orthodox in the Muslim faith, he aimed at modifying social customs in accordance with western ideas, and more especially at introducing the philanthropic principles which had not been very prominent under older Muslim conditions. As Sir Valentine Chirol remarks of Egypt: " Except within the narrow limits of good deeds prescribed by the Koran, which the old-fashioned orthodox Mahommedan considers himself bound to perform, the philanthrophy which at home maintains hospitals, endows schools and colleges, promotes housing of the poor, etc., is almost unknown amongst the Egyptian educated classes" (Sir Val. Chirol: *The Egyptian Problem*, p. 171). Sir Valentine Chirol does not note to how great an extent this is of recent growth in the west, and where it is not recent, as in the endowment of schools and colleges, it has its parallel in Islam, if anything, indeed, a more generous parallel. But the eighteenth and nineteenth centuries certainly saw a great humanitarian wave passing over the west, and it was this which Sir Sayyid Ahmed Khan desired to reproduce in the east. His views were expressed in a periodical which he named *Tahzibu l-Akhlaq* " The Reform of Morals." But he was not solely interested in education and philanthropy, he was concerned with theology as well, and in this he showed a liberal and modernist attitude very similar to that which has produced a considerable ferment in Christian theology, and for the freedom of his speculations in this direction he was declared excommunicate by the leading authorities of Islam, the " learned men " whose views command more or less consideration.

As a result of this disowning by the stricter Muslims Sir Sayyid Ahmed Rhan and his followers came forth as a distinctly sectarian body of liberal Muslims who appear in the returns of the Indian census as *necharis* or *naturis* and, later on, these identified themselves with the Mu'tazilites, the rationalists of the early days of the 'Abbasid Khalifs. Since the death of Sir Sayyid his work has been carried on by the *Mawlawi Chiragh 'Ali* and then by the *Rt. Hon. Sayyid 'Amir 'Ali* who has expressed the later attitude of the necharis in his " Spirit of Islam " (Calcutta, 1890). In the earlier phases of this movement the tendency was distinctly towards rationailsm, but its later developments have swung round to orthodox Islam and to the position of loyalty to the Qur'an alone as the authoritative code of religion and have thus assumed a semi-puritan position. In this, however, it differs very much from the tendencies of the Wahhabis : it does not seek to revive the primitive life and discipline of Islam, but only to place the text of the Qur'an in a position of pre-eminent authority to the exclusion of all later tradition and canon law. The development of this purely Qur'anic theology necessarily resulted in the isolation of what we may term the " left wing " of the movement, of those who, having started on the path towards rationalism, were unable to turn in a reactionary direction, and this, the smaller, section of the Nechari movement has its representative in *Khuda Bukhsh* and his " Essays, Indian and Islamic " (London, 1912). In connection with this movement also must be mentioned the work of *Hakim Ajmal Haziqu l-Mulk* of Delhi, who has devoted himself to training graduates of the college at Aligarh and sending them out as mission preachers and mawlawis to spread a strictly Qur'anic theology, a kind of reformed Muslim teaching, amongst young men of the educated classes.

Independent of Sir Sayyid Ahmad Khan was the movement known as the *Anjuman-i-Himayet-i-Islam* of Lahore, founded in 1885, a missionary society on lines copied from those of the Christian missonary organisations working in India. It maintains schools for the poorer classes and orphanages; it publishes a monthly missionary magazine, as well as numerous booklets and tracts of orthodox character, but with a strong tincture of liberalism in theology and with a marked tendency towards social reform. At a later date the society opened a book-store at Lahore for the circulation of Qur'ans and apologetic literature. All this work, though based on Christian precedents, is mainly Sunni in character.

In 1894 a similar missionary society called the *Nadwatu 'Ulama* was established at Lucknow, and also produces its missionary magazine. In 1898, however, this society took a more definitely educational line by founding a college, the *Daru l-'Ulum*, at Lucknow, and later on this developed branch institutions at Madras and Shahjanpur. These colleges are on western lines, modern and and efficient, and at the same time strictly Muslim in their religious teaching : they act as seminaries for the production of missionary preachers who are said to exercise considerable influence amongst young men of western education.

Another college, the *Madrasa-i-Ilahiyat*, has been founded at Cawnpore which is specially concerned with work intended to counteract the activity of the Arya Samaj, the Hindu modernist sect.

A quite different history stands behind the sect known as the *Ahmadiya* which arose in the Panjab, partly, perhaps, as a reaction against Christian missionary activity there, has spread through India, and extended its operations to England, Syria, and Egypt. As the one section of Islam which has made efforts to gain converts in England it is particularly interesting. The Babists, it is true, have also established missions in England and America, but they, though historically connected with Islam, can in no sense be regarded as a Muslim sect. In its general tendencies the

Ahmadiya takes a middle path between orthodoxy and the rationalism of the Necharis, but has certain peculiar characteristics due to the teaching of its founder about himself. The founder, Mirza Ghulam Ahmad was born in 1838, began to teach in 1879, and died in 1908. He claimed to be the Mahdi, who is generally regarded as the precurser of the Messiah, but by a development which does not occur elsewhere in Muslim theology, he identified the Madhi with the Messiah and taught that he himself as Mahdi-Messiah fulfilled the religious expectations of both Muslims and Christians. At a later period he further identified himself with the Avatar of the Hindus, so that in his teaching we find a distinct effort to comprehend all these religions in one system, a tendency which appears in the Babist doctrine as well and perhaps marks the probable line of future development of liberal Islam, the tendency namely to present it as a simple monotheism in which orthodox Islam, Christianity, and a reformed Hinduism such as appears in the teaching of the Arya Samaj can he be fused: the idea that all religions express the same fundamental truths in spite of divergences in detail. This tendency underlies a great deal of Sufi or mystic teaching.

A large part of Mirza Ghulam Ahmad's teaching aimed at a reconciliation of Christianity and Islam. Christ Himself had foretold a second advent and promised that he would send a *paraclete* to continue his work. Interpreting this *paraclete* as "the famous one," i.e., reading *peri-*

clytes for *paraclytes*, as is actually done sometimes in early Christian literature, he held that this promise was fulfilled in himself since the name *Ahmad* bears the meaning of "famous." The same argument was used by the Prophet Muhammad whose name was susceptible of the same rendering, and it was probably from that that Mirza Ghulam Ahmad derived his own theory. It has a weak point, for Ghulam Ahmad means the slave of the famous one," and does not justify the use of Ahmad as in the nominative.

The life of Christ is not fully treated in the Qur'an. In one passage (Qur. 3.48) a reference seems to be made to the death and subsequent ascension of Christ, " Remember when God said, O Jesus, verily I will cause thee to die and will take thee up to myself and deliver thee from the unbelievers: but another passage (Qur. 4.156) distinctly states that Christ was not crucified, " And for their saying, Verily we havs slain Christ, Jesus the Son of Mary, the Apostle of God:— yet they slew him not, they had only his likeness." This reproduces the Gnostic idea that at the last moment Christ was delivered from His enemies and Simon (or Jude) substituted in His stead, and that is the usual teaching held by orthodox Muslims. Mirza Ghulam Ahmad introduted a new interpretation which might be regarded as reconciling these two passages and one in which he was, perhaps, influenced by modern writers on the resurrection. He held that Christ was crucified, but did not actually die on the cross; He was taken down in a swoon, recovered from His wounds, and travelled to India where He died and was buried at Srinagar in Kashmir. This teaching differs very considerably from the legendary account given in the *Qisasu l-Anbiya*, " Stories of the Prophets " and similar works, but shows a knowledge of current Christian controversial literature. The Qur'an very plainly refers to the miraculous nature of the conception and birth of Christ (cf. Qur. 19. 22-34 : 23. 52) and this Mirza Ghulam Ahmad admits, but considers that the admission does not prove the deity of Christ : learned physicians of the Greek and Indian schools, he says, have " shown the possibility of a child being formed in the mother's womb without the seed of man " (*Review of Religions*, 1.72).

It was in March, 1889, that Mirza Ghulam Ahmad first declared that he was entitled to *bai'at* or " homage " from Muslims, but it was not until 1891 when he declared that he fulfilled the prophecies relating to the Mahdi and the Messiah that his followers began to form a distinct sect and refused to take part in the worship held in the mosques. When the government of India took the census of 1900 they were, at their own request, entered under the heading of Ahmadiya in the returns. According to that census they were reckoned at 13,131 males. They are now estimated at about 70,000 in all.

Ahmad died in 1908 and was succeeded by Hakim Nuru d-Din as the first Khalifa, and he was assisted by a committee known as the *Sadr-*

Anjuman-i-Ahmadiya " Head Society of the Ahmadiya " on general lines rather resembling the other liberal movements which we have already mentioned. In 1913, however, symptoms of internal division began to appear. Mirza Ghulam Ahmad had strictly enjoined his followers to abstain from any form of political agitation, an injunction which Sayyid Ahmad Khan had also laid on his society, but in that year a very widespread disturbance was aroused by the action of the government in proposing to remove a portion of a mosque at Cawnpore which stood in the way of certain road improvements and in the controversy which raged round this, Khwajah Kamal ad-Din, a prominent member of the Ahmadiya, took a leading part. Some of his fellow members resented this as disloyalty to the founder's directions, and his action was severely criticised by Mirza Bashiru d- Din Mahmad Ahmad, the eldest son of Mirza Ghulam Ahmad by his second wife, in the Urdu periodical *Alfazal*. Others of the community were annoyed by this protest which seemed to them an unwarrantable assumption of authority by Mirza Bashiru-d-Din on the ground of his relationship to the founder, and thus a schism arose. At Nuru-d-Din's death those who opposed Khwajah Kamal ad-Din's action elected Mirza Bashiru d-Din as Khalifa at Qadian, the headquarters of the sect. but those who had disapproved of his criticism of Khwaja Kamal ad-Din seceded and founded a new society, the *Anjuman Isha 'at-i-Islam* or " Society for the spread of Islam" at Lahore. The Qadian branch maintain that Mirza Ghulam Ahmad was truly a prophet and denounce all those who do not recognise his prophetic claims as *kafirs* or "unbelievers." The Lahore party recognise him to have been Mahdi and Messiah, but not as a prophet, an office which, they assert, he never actually claimed, and they are not willing to regard other Muslims as unbelievers even though they do not admit Ahmadiya doctrine. Thus the two groups represent the extremer advocates of the sacred character of the founder and the more moderate adherents who have developed more on liberal lines. But both have shown themselves keen supporters of western methods of education and vigorous in the production of periodical and controversial literature, and thus both appear as active missionary workers for the extension of Islam. The *Sadr-Anjuman* continues to be the controlling body of the Qadian party, and has shown great activity in educational work. It maintains a flourishing high school at Qadian which is affiliated to the Panjab University as well as a theological college with a seven year course for the training of missionaries. Primary schools also have been established, as well as several schools for girls. It issues a number of vernacular periodicals and an English monthly *The Review of Religions*. Beside the original *Anjuman* which is thus mainly associated with educational work on western lines, there is a more definitely religious society the *Anjuman Taraqqi-i-Islam* founded by the present Khalifa and engaged in missionary work. Mission preachers have been sent to different parts of India and, it is said, to Syria, Egypt, and England, but no details appear to be available as to their work which, of course, is quite distinct from that of the Lahore branch. This missionary society has commenced the publication of a Qur'an with transliteration into Roman letters which will be " a radical help to the new converts to Islam who have to learn by heart a portion of the Holy Qur'an to be read in prayers," as well as a translation into English, and very full notes explanatory of the Ahmadiya interpretation of the Qur'an. The first part of this edition appeared in 1915, and the whole is to be complete in thirty parts: it does not seem that anything more than the first part can as yet be procured. The covers of the part contain a general summary of Ahmadiya teaching from which the following passage may be quoted: "The Holy Prophet (may peace and blessings of God be upon him) called the Promised One 'Isa' or Jesus, son of Mary. This did not mean that the very Jesus, who appeared in the world 1900 years ago, would come back again. As many as thirty verses of the Holy Qur'an may be quoted to show that Jesus is dead, and it is clear that the dead cannot come back to this world. Even the tomb of Jesus may be seen in the Khanyar Street, Srinagar, Kashmir, where He came to deliver His message to the lost tribes of Israel, who had settled in Afghanistan and Cashmere. The Promised one was to be Jesus in the same sense in which John the Baptist was Elijah, *i.e.*, he was to appear in the spirit and character of Jesus, son of Mary, just as John the Baptist appeared in the spirit and character of Elijah." This promised One, the Mahdi-Messiah, was Mirza Ghulam Ahmad whose message was not for Muslims only, but was to reveal the truth to men of all religions and so was foretold, under different names, in the sacred books of the Christians, Zoroastrians, Buddhists, and others.

The separatist body of Lahore has also distinguished itself by its activity in educational work, the chief institution of this sort being the Muslim High School of Lahore which was opened in 1916, and it has its own periodicals, including the *Islamic Review* published at Woking, in Surrey, where the representative and missionary in England, Khwajah Kamal ad-Din has been established since August, 1914. The Mosque at Woking was of earlier date, and erected by the late Professor Leitner, formerly Principal of the Oriental College, Lahore, and at his death was given by his heirs to the Ahmadiya body. Khwaja Kamal ad-Din, whose action in 1913 had led to the schism, though no doubt the rival tendencies were bound to produce separation sooner or later, had been working in England since 1912, and it was from England that he had joined in the controversy about the proposed interference with the mosque at Cawnpore. The Lahore section of the Ahmadiya is not much occupied with efforts to convert other Muslims and has drawn closer to the orthodox community; it chief activity is in the attempt to commend Islam to non-Muslims, and tries to commend a liberal type of Muslim teaching as a reasonable religion for the western world. Apparently about 200 English converts have been made and the society has made efforts to care for the religious and moral welfare of Indian Muslim students in England. An effort is being made to erect a mosque in London where the Ahmadiya already possess a meeting-room for prayer and instruction which has been recently moved from Notting Hill to Hampstead.

The Ahmadiya movement is the indirect result of the great ferment produced in the religious life of India by three great forces, the British Government, Christian missionary propaganda, and the work of various European orientalists, all co-operating in bringing western thought into touch with India. These western influences told first on the Hindus and Parsis, and only touched Islam at a rather later date, but they ultimately did tell, and the younger generation of Muslims could no longer ignore the solvent influence of modern thought, of the methods of historical criticism partially introduced by Christian controversial treatises and more fully developed and applied by orientalists, and of the spread of modern scientific enquiry brought about by the establishment of schools on western lines and the necessity of those who aspired to government employ making themselves acquainted with this new thought. Sir Sayyid Ahmad Khan and his followers came under the same influences and simply tried to re-adjust their point of view in the light of the new knowledge, an attitude only likely to commend itself to those who had felt these influences and not to the rank and file. Mirza Ghulam Ahmad became, in a sense, the apostle of liberal Islam and presented it in a form mingled with mystical and purely oriental elements which, however, unfamiliar to western minds, are the time-honoured accompaniments of constructive missionary work in Indian thought, and bear traces of the Persian influences which have already pervaded North West India. Taken out of this environment the movement resolves itself mainly into liberal Islam with the peculiarity that it has a definitely propagandist spirit and feels confident that it can make an appeal to western nations, an appeal which has already been made with some measure of success. If it be thought that this success be insignificant it must be remembered that missionary progress in India, where the Muslim community is now the largest in the world, was slow; it has won one-fifth of the population there, and this has taken three times as long as it took Christianity to spread through the Roman Empire. Rapidity of progress is not always the most reassuring sign in missionary work. But the Ahmadiya movement in England does not only aim at making converts, though it invites them: it is making a very definite effort to improve the attitude of the English people towards Islam and to secure for it a fair and just hearing, a purpose which must command sympathy even from those who are actively engaged in Christian missionary work amongst Muslims, for the removal of misrepresentation and misunderstanding can only be a gain to both sides in controversy. Unfortunately, like most mission work, the Ahmadiya seems to suffer from the zeal of imprudent advocates who obviously base special pleading upon strained interpretations of history. It is impossible to present the Arabs of the time of the Prophet as enlightened moderns of western education, and perhaps a more prudent policy would be to face more fully the fact of historical development and social evolution which is true of all human society and sufficiently accounts for the peculiarities and survivals which occur in Islam as in every other religion.

CHAPTER V

THE SHI'ITE REACTION ON THE WEST: THE BABIST MOVEMENT

THE Shi'ite branch of Islam, as has been already noted (p. 9, &c., above), believed that the Church of Islam has been placed by God under the guidance of Imams who were incarnations of the Holy Spirit which at the death of each Imam passed to his successor so that in one sense they formed a legitimist hereditary succession, though in another sense they might be regarded as all the same, the same spirit being tabernacled in each in turn. Of these Imams 'Ali was the first, and he continued and indeed completed the work of the Prophet. From the Shi'ite point of view the first three Khalifs were usurpers, unjustly intervening to prevent 'Ali from doing the work which God had entrusted to him, and the cursing of those three is one of the distinctive marks of the Shi'ite. 'Ali himself, the first Iman, was the fourth Khalif and then for a while Islam was ruled righteously, but at his death the 'Umayyad Mua'wiya usurped the Khalifate and ever since the Sunni community, in communion with the Khalif, has been in schism and lacks divine guidance. As to the succession

THE SHI'ITE REACTION

after 'Ali the Shi'ites are divided amongst themselves, but the largest branch, the *Ithna'ashariya* or " Twelvers," which is the state religion of Persia, believes that there were in all twelve Imams, 'Ali, his two sons, Hasan and Husayn, in turn, and then nine descendants of Husayn, of whom the last was Muhammed al-Muntazir, who took part in the funeral of his father in A.H. 260 (A.D. 873) and then disappeared and was seen no more. For some time, however, the community was guide by a teacher who was known as the *Bab* or " door " and who was believed to be in constant communication with the concealed Imam. The fourth, and last, of the *Babs* died in A.H. 940-1, and then the Twelvers remained without a visible head on earth.

At the beginning of the nineteenth century, A.D., a religious revival took place amongst the Persian Shi'ites; it is tempting to conjecture some community of origin with the contemporary Wahhabis, but no solid ground for supposing such a connection exists. The leader of this revival was the Sheikh Ahmad al-Ahsa'i (born 1733, died 1826) and its characteristic teaching was that there must be some earthly representation of the Imam acting as an intermediary between him and his people. The adherents of this theory were known as the Shaykhi school and were accepted by other Shi'ites of the " Twelver " sect as perfectly orthodox. They regarded the Sheikh Ahmad himself as the representative, inspired, not directly by God as a prophet would be, but by revelation from the holy

Spirit incarnate in the Imam who had been some 900 years in concealment. The Sheikh was followed by two successors, the Sheikh Ahmad, and then Sayyid Kizim, the latter dying in 1844. None of these used the title *Bab*, but were regarded by their followers as discharging very much the same functions as the *Babs* of earlier date.

At the death of the third leader of the Shaykhi school in 1844 a young man named Mirza 'Ali Muhammad came forward and began to preach these same doctrines, claiming himself to be the intermediary between the concealed Imam and his people and assuming the title of *Bab* which had been in use amongst the earlier Shi'ites. This year A.D. 1844 was 1260 of the Hijra, exactly 1000 years after the disappearance of the Twelfth Imam, and there seems to have been a popular belief that the period of concealment would endure for a thousand years. The claims of the young preacher found a ready response and he very soon had a large body of followers who looked upon him as the herald of a new age which would soon see the return of the Imam to earth and the establishment of a reign of righteousness. The actual use of the title *Bab*, however, annoyed the religious authorities, and the preaching of a new era in which the existing state would pass away and God's saints rule on earth alarmed the secular officials, and so efforts were made to put down the Babists by force, with the result that there were armed risings of the sect in various parts, and the Shah's government had much difficulty in dealing with them. The Babists were bitterly hostile to the reigning dynasty, and openly declared that it was their aim to replace it by a theocracy in which the Bab would be, at least for a time, the Imam's vicar. A considerable part of Mirza 'Ali's life, after the commencement of his public ministry, was passed in imprisonment in which he was sometimes treated with severity, more often with consideration and respect, and in 1850 he was executed, still a young man, probably not more than thirty years of age. During the latter part of his life he transferred the title of *Bab* to one of his followers and himself assumed that of *Qa'im*, the traditional title of the Imam restored to earth, that is to say, a re-incarnation of the Holy Spirit which had been transmitted from 'Ali to his eleven successors.

He was followed by a youth named Mirza Yahya on whom he had conferred the name of *Subh-i-Azel* or "dawn of eternity," the son of Mirza Buzurg of Nur, who had left home and become one of the most devoted members of the Babist sect, but, as he was too young to guide the temporal affairs of the community these were entrusted to his half-brother Baha'ullah. For a couple of years things proceeded peaceably, though the sect continued to be regarded with grave suspicion by the government, and remained in a state of simmering insurrection. In 1852 two Babists made an attempt to assassinate the Shah Nasiru d-Din. It is certain that this attempt, which was not successful, was not made with the knowledge or consent of the responsible leaders of the sect but was the rash act of two fanatics. It was, however, the immediate occasion of a ferocious attack upon the Babist community whose members were hunted down, tortured, and slaughtered in large numbers. At the time, undoubtedly, the Babists were a formidable menace to the government and the ruling dynasty, conscious of its disrepute and unpopularity, was very seriously frightened. Then, as always, fear begat cruelty and the persecution of 1852 is one of the darkest episodes of the history of Persia. Mirza Yahya and his half-brother escaped and took refuge in Baghdad which became the headquarters of the sect for the twelve years 1852–1864, and there they lived under Turkish protection though in touch with their concealed followers in Persia. As time went on, however, repeated complaints were made by Persia to the Turkish government; Baghdad was too near the sacred shrines of Kerbela, the place of Husayn's martyrdom, and Najaf, the reputed burial place of 'Ali, cities visited every year by vast numbers of Persian pilgrims, who were thus brought into easy contact with those whom the Persian government regarded as its most dangerous enemies. In 1864, therefore, the Bab and his companions were removed to Constantinople, and a few months later, to Adrianople where they remained for a little more than four years (1864–1868).

During the Baghdad period Baha'ullah, the half-brother and steward of Subh-i-Azel, had

THE SHI‘ITE REACTION

withdrawn for a while to Kurdistan for the purpose of religious meditation. Then at Adrianople in 1866 he began to proclaim that he was the "One whom God shall reveal" to whom Mirza 'Ali had borne witness, the Messiah of whom the Bab was the precurser. This new development was vigorously opposed to by Subh-i-Azel, and the community was divided into two rival factions which at length came to open warfare until the Turkish authorities found it necessary to interpose and exile Subh-i-Azel to Cyprus and Baha'ullah to 'Akka in Syria. The branch in Cyprus was the smaller body, and from this time ceases to have any great importance; Subh-i-Azel was a quiet and retiring man of deep personal piety, and for the most part lived secluded from his followers. Baha'ullah was of more vigorous personality, and his sect, the Baha'is, became more prominent and influential. He ruled his followers at 'Akka from 1868 to 1892. Professor Browne says: "That the Baha'is is constituted a great potential political force in Persia when I was there in 1887-8 was to me self-evident. Their actual numbers were considerable (Lord Curzon estimated them at the time he wrote at nearer a million than half a million souls), their intelligence and social position were above the average, they were particularly well represented in the postal and telegraph services, they were well disciplined and accustomed to yield a ready devotion and obedience to their spiritual leaders, and their attitude towards the secular and ecclesiastical rulers of Persia was, hostile or at least indifferent. Any Power which by conciliating their Supreme Pontiff at 'Akka, could have made use of this organisation in Persia might have established an enormous influence in that country." (Browne: *Materials for the Study of the Babi Religion*, Cambridge, 1918, p.xvi.) It seems that the Russian government, and possibly also the British, were disposed to conciliate Baha' ullah, " The Russian Government showed a good deal of civility to the Baha'is of 'Ishqabad (Askabad), where they were allowed or encouraged them to build a *Mashri-qu' l-Adhkar*, or place of worship, which was, I believe, the first of its kind ever erected." (id.p.xvii.) The Baha'is themselves state that the British Consul-General at Baghdad about 1859 invited the Baha'is to place themselves under British protection.

At Baha'ullah's death in 1892 a new schism took place, the Baha'is being divided into two parties (i) the followers of Baha'ullah's eldest son 'Abbas Effendi who held that the divine revelation was not ended, and that the Holy Spirit which had inspired Baha'ullah had descended upon his son, and (ii) the followers of a younger son named Mirza Muhammad 'Ali who believed that it had ended and were content with the truths revealed through Baha'ullah. In the Persian revolution of 1908 the Azalis, as the followers of Subh-i-Azel are called, took a leading part in the insurrection, and since then seem to have thrown in their lot with the Nationalists, whilst the Baha'is sided with the reactionaries.

THE SHI'ITE REACTION

In 1893 a Baha'i missionary named Khayru'llah, an adherent of the more extreme section led by 'Abbas Effendi, reached America and began to preach in Chicago, which very soon became the head quarters of a vigorous Baha'i community and the seat of a Baha'i Publishing Society" which issued English translations of a number of Babist works. This effort went on quietly and steadily for five years, branches were established in New York, Philadelphia, Ithaca, Kansas, and elsewhere. About 1895 Khayru'llah married an English wife, Miss Marian Miller. In 1898 he visited England and France, founding branches of the Baha'i society in each of these countries, and finally reached 'Akka with sixteen American visitors. In part this was intended to be a pious pilgrimage to visit 'Abbas Effendi and to see the burial place of Baha'ullah, and in part it was an effort to obtain more accurate knowledge of certain holy verses revealed by Baha'ullah of which Khayru'llah had not yet been able to get a precise account, and to which, he feared, his teaching might not conform. 'Abbas Effendi expressed his approval of all Khayru'llah's teaching, but steadily avoided discussing doctrine with him. As this at length became significant Khayru'llah began to discuss the matter with other Baha'is at 'Akka and before long discovered that 'Abbas Effendi's teaching had developed on lines quite different from those which he had hitherto accepted and taught. At length Khayru'llah " found no escape from abandoning 'Abbas Effendi and joined the rival subsection of the Baha'is who followed Mirza Muhammad 'Ali, and thus at the present time the American Baha'i body is itself divided between those who adhere to 'Abbas Effendi and those who recognise the leadership of Mirza Muhammad 'Ali.

In the course of its evolution Baha'ism has travelled far from the Shi'ite source in which it had its beginning, and as Shi'ism itself contains many elements widely remote from pure Islam it is dubious whether Baha'ism has now any claim to be regarded as Muslim, although it is historically an off-shoot from the main trunk of Islam. The Baha'is deny miracles, asserting that the production of a revelation is in itself sufficient to establish and justify their claims; they deny a bodily resurrection, and prefer the doctrine of *raj'at* or "return," a modified form of transmigration, from which as a logical result they do not accept the doctrine of a future life in heaven or hell, so that on these points they differ very materially from the orthodox teaching of Islam; accepting and honouring the Qur'an they are also prepared to accept the Old and New Testaments, indeed these figure much more prominently than the Qur'an in the tracts they publish in America, and they do not hold, like other Muslims, that these are so corrupt as to be of no spiritual utility. They have developed, in fact, a kind of undenominational religion which seeks to combine Christianity, Judaism, and Islam on lines which commend themselves to the latitudinarian attitude at present characteristic of western thought ; the theory of a divine incarnation in the head of the sect has very much faded into the background and the American and English branches can hardly be recognised as the spiritual descendants of the fierce sectaries who in 1848-50 made so formidable a revolt against the Persian government. The ethical teaching of the Baha'is is unexceptional, if somewhat lacking in vigour ; and as thought has developed in American surroundings it has tended towards pacifism, internationalism, and feminism. To some extent this shows a drifting ; it has absorbed ready-made ideas which do not rise spontaneously from its primitive teaching, and one may question how far it is likely to be a factor of any great weight in western thought, although it has undoubtedly contributed towards helping the west to picture Islam as a possible religion and to learn from it, though of course converts to Baha'ism are not accepted by Muslims as brothers in the faith. As regards its future in Asia, that is another matter ; there, and especially in Persia, it still seems to have great power, even though at the moment that power is latent, and it is quite possible that it may yet play a part in political events, perhaps as a reactionary force against democracy, though certainly not in support of the dynastic claims of the Shahs of Persia.

CHAPTER VI

PAN-ISLAMIC HOPES AND NATIONALISM

THE earlier sectarian divisions of Islam appear to us rather as political than religious movements. This was inevitable from the nature of Islam which is essentially a community rather on the lines of Free-masonry than of a religious denomination as understood in Western Europe. Loyalty to the Prophet and his " successor " was so obviously a primary duty that the honest dissenter was compelled to maintain by some plausible argument that the one who claimed to be the Prophet's " successor " actually was not so, or that the office was one which could be dispensed with. But the point of constitutional law could not be ignored : it could not be maintained that there ever had been a Muslim community without a visible and temporal head or deputy acting for such a head, and so every non-conformist had to give some reason to justify his schism from the Church of Islam. The ideal of a close brotherhood of all believers is at all times implied.

In the latter part of the nineteenth century two movements took place which bear very direct relationship to this theory. In the first place we have the "Pan-Islamic" movement which was an attempt to realize that fraternity more fully and to get rid of the obstacle caused by schism wherever the barriers of heresy were not so great as to debar the separated bodies from a common life; it was, in fact, a genuine effort to reform Islam by emphasizing one of its oldest and most impressive claims. The other movement, diametrically opposed to this, was the "Nationalist" which sought unity of communal life and interest in the fortuitous group we call a "nation"; ignoring racial and religious differences it sought to unify the elements whose only common feature is their subjection to the same political control. This was opposed to all the traditions of Islam and introduced an entirely new idea of western origin.

The history of the "Pan-Islamic Movement" is connected with the career of the Sultan Abdu l-Hamid (A.D. 1876–1908) who became to a great extent its patron, and seems to have regarded it as a bulwark against nationalism and western influences generally. At his accession Turkey was on the verge of war with Russia, and the parliamentary government and liberal ministry which was then in power and striving to westernize Turkey was unable to prevent the war which ended disastrously for the Turks. As a result the government was discredited in the eyes of the people, and, taking advantage of this, the Sultan dismissed it and seized control himself, beginning to rule as an autocrat in the old fashion, apparently with the warm approval of his subjects who were glad to see an end of an experiment which had brought so much misfortune upon the country. This autocratic rule began in 1878 and continued until his deposition in 1908. Very early in this period he made it his policy to put himself forward as the champion of Islam, and endeavoured to gather round himself every movement which tended to make for the solidarity of Islam, regarding himself as the legitimate leader in his function as Khalif.

The western world first began to take note of this policy about 1883, and from that time onward a note of alarm begins to be sounded which becomes more pronounced as we approach the twentieth century. But for the most part the West tended to misunderstand the nature of the movement and to suppose that the Khalif was a kind of Muslim Pope, and even to hope that he might be employed as a kind of tool to manipulate the world of Islam The note of anxiety, however, was sufficiently clear to commend the movement to the Muslim community at large; if it were the cause of disquiet to the nations of Christendom, that fact sufficed to rally round it many whose feelings were anti-European. There is no question that Abdu l-Hamid spent a great deal of time, trouble, and money in organizing the Pan-Islamic movement and in sending out missionaries to all parts of the Muslim world, and it seems probable that by these means he was more widely recognised as Khalif than any of his immediate predecessors. The most important part of a Khalif's recognition consists in the formal mention of his name in the *khutba* or prayer before the Friday sermon, and he was thus mentioned in the mosques of India which had not been done for any of the Turkish Sultans before him, and to this the British Government made no objection, indeed the tendency was rather to encourage the full recognition of the Sultan's Khalifate and to rely upon the power of bringing pressure to bear upon him so that he might be forced to check unpromising developments amongst those who recognised his authority. This was simply an attempt to repeat with Islam the policy which had already been tried more than once successfully with the Christian Church, but it had the fatal defect that Muslim conditions differ entirely from Christian, and that the Khalif still possessed enough temporal power to be formidable, and was able to play off one Western power against another. How far Abdu l-Hamid achieved any real results beyond increased prestige it is difficult to say. The liberal element in Islam for the most part held aloof from him, estranged by his reactionary policy; and the most vigorous reforming movements, those of the Wahhabis and Sanusi, would have nothing at all to do with him, and did not even recognise him as Khalif.

The pan-Islamic movement found its leader in Abdu l-Hamid, and for this he was pre-eminently fitted by his office, but the real brains of the movement were in *Jemal ad-Din* (d.1896). He was born early in the nineteenth century at Asadabad near Hamadan in Persia, but was of Afghan descent. He had travelled widely in Muslim lands and was inspired by an intense loyalty to his religion, a kind of patriotism closely parallel to that which has produced national liberators, and his ideas still exercise a profound influence in the world of Islam. He held that there were two great nations, the Muslim and the Christian, engaged in a relentless struggle in which Christendom is at present the aggressor: the fanatical spirit which produced the Crusades still continues and, however much disguised, is still the motive power behind western politics; it gives the impetus which urges those powers to perpetual aggressions on Islam, and which shows itself in European literature in constant hatred, abuse, and ridicule of the religion of Islam. Before this relentless opposition the Muslims have no chance unless they unite in self-defence, and it is urgently necessary that the whole community rally to the support of any part attacked. Jemal ad-Din does not appear to have been interested in theological questions, and took no part in any of the modernist movements of his time, but confined his attention to arousing a spirit of patriotism amongst Muslims.

In India he was treated as an agitator, and had to leave the country. In 1880 he was in Egypt, and threw himself heart and soul into Arabi Pasha's revolt. Professedly this was an anti-Turkish agitation, but Jemal ad-Din associated himself with it as an effort to shake off western control which lay heavy upon the country. In 1882 the British expelled him from Egypt, and he passed over to Constantinople where he was well received by Abdu l-Hamid, and there he lived until his death fourteen years later, and during that time he gave a clearer form and direction to the Sultan's pan-Islamic policy.

The revolution of 1908 meant the downfall of pan-Islamic ideals in the presence of their rival, the spirit of nationalism. For the next ten years those ideas were under eclipse, but after the war they revived in a slightly changed form, and will certainly claim serious attention in the near future.

Nationalism shows the influence of theories quite strange to, and indeed subversive of, Islam. The Prophet endeavoured to unite his followers in a close brotherhood wherein all rivalries of tribe or family would be laid aside, and when Islam spread to other lands this brotherhood was still maintained, and was held to over-pass all barriers of race or language. The idea of national unities as apart from the claims of common religion and ignoring the religious differences of the constituent individuals is of western origin, alien in its character, and anti-Muslim in its tendency. So far as Turkish nationality is concerned it is of recent date and directly due to the suggestions of western ethnologists, for it was such suggestions and not any racial consciousness which first roused an idea of kinship amongst the Turks, and for some time it was confined to a small literary clique whith had its nucleus at Salonika.

In the beginning its scope was confined to the Othmanli Turks, then it was extended to all the Turkish race, and finally to the whole group of Turanians as they are classified by ethnologists. It was not nationalism in the stricter sense but rather a racial grouping on the lines rendered familiar by German writers of the late nineteenth and early twentieth century, lines which have not yet commanded universal assent for conscious racial loyalty is a recent and artificial development, and it aimed at embracing those fairly considerable Turkish elements in Central Asia which were under Russian rule, and so, more or less consciously, it tended to increase the anti-Russian feeling already strong in Turkey. The whole programme of the Turkish party was opposed to the ideals of pan-Islam, and the party was viewed with much disfavour by Abdu l-Hamid for which reason, perhaps, it seemed a congenial refuge for many who were discontented with his régime.

Abdu l-Hamid's reign ended at the revolution of 1908. The "Young Turk" party deposed Abdu l-Hamid and established Muhammad as Sultan to reign on constitutional lines with the help of a parliament. At first this was a nationalist government in the western sense, as it sought to incorporate all those who lived under the Sultan's rule, and thus dealt with a community whose only bond of cohesion lay in its political government, but before long the racial theories of the Turkish party which formed a weighty majority amongst the Young Turks, and included those who were the most vocal and ready to participate in political activity began to dominate the policy of the state. Like every revolution a good deal that happened in the Turkish revolt of 1908 was lucky accident on the one side together with accidental mistakes on the other. Perhaps the general feeling was against Abdu l-Hamid, at least amongst the population of Constantinople where there was a large Levantine element, and the action of the capital carried the provinces, but it is not at all clear that his deposition can be rightly described as an act meeting with the approval of the people at large. Amongst those who opposed him there was great diversity of opinion, but the actual movement, led by the " Committee of Union and Progress," was in the hands of the nationalists, the only section of the community organised politically and in a position to voice its grievances, and, still more, the only one which had any clear policy to propose. The Young Turks preached the brotherhood and equality of all the subjects of the Sultan, and the inauguration of the new government was hailed with an outburst of enthusiasm and the ostentatious fraternizing of Muslims, Greeks, Armenians, and Jews who were for the future to live in concord and brotherly love.

Very soon, however, entirely different influences began to appear. The new government began to be dominated by the adherents of the pan-Turkish theory, and aimed at welding all the diverse elements into a Turkish whole. The apostle of these Turkish ideas was Ziya Gok Alp, and the home of the movement was in Salonika where it had its expression in a local paper called *Genj Kalemlar*, " the Young Writer." The aim and policy of the movement was largely literary, an attempt was made to get rid of Arabic and Persian words from the Turkish language, and to invent native terms to take their place, and even to translate the Qur'an into Turkish. The more advanced section, whose programme is expressed in Tekin Alp's *Turkish and Pan-Turkish Ideal* (cf. Admiralty War Staff, *I.D.*, 1153) tried to maintain that even the religious ideas of the Turks were superior to those of the Arabs, so that there was a kind of Turkish super-Islam which greatly surpassed the traditional sort revealed through an Arabic medium. These ideas received their chief opposition from the *Islamji* or Muslim party because they were definitely subversive of orthodox Islam.

The acclaimed theory that all Turkish subjects were to enjoy complete political equality, and were to live together as brothers, irrespective of religious and racial differences was received with almost hysterical enthusiasm, but that enthusiasm was short-lived. The abolition of religious distinctions in the treatment of the community meant that Christians became liable for military service equally with Muslims, instead of being exempt as heretofore : no doubt the Greeks and others were perfectly justified in stating that they did not object to military service *per se*, but only to service in the army as actually constituted, but it can hardly be doubted that the prospect of service, even in a reformed army, involving very possibly temporary exile to the dreaded deserts of Arabia, would hardly be congenial to the Levantine merchants. Hitherto each religious community had enjoyed a considerable degree of autonomy in such matters as marriage laws, the law of succession, etc., and regarded these liberties with great jealousy, but the new government proposed to bring them all under new state-made laws. This was introducing state control in a fashion strange to the east, though usual in the western countries; in India the British Government has always been careful to recognise the right of each religious body to its own laws on all such matters as these; the law is administered in the ordinary civil court, but the legal authorities recognised are those of the sect and the jurists of that sect are consulted; but the Young Turks had learned their legal theories from Lyons rather than from India, and proposed a complete westernization of jurisprudence in a country which did not admit of it. The Muslims admit polygamy, Christians do not: Muslims allow free discretion of divorce to either party, subject only to restrictions imposed by the terms of the marriage contract; whilst the eastern churches, though not taking so strict a view as the Christians in the west, yet make divorce rare and difficult. The attempt to re-cast all the traditional laws and usages of the subject groups, often in matters which were regarded as of religious sanction, roused intense opposition, which, however, had to be very cautiously expressed, as the home policy of the Young Turks was, if anything, considerably more severe than that of Abdu l-Hamid: indeed the people soon found that they had exchanged a tyrant who was easy-going in matters which did not affect his own personal authority for one which went out of its way to interfere vexatiously in all manner of matters which had usually been respected even by the most domineering autocrats. Probably there can be no more troublesome tyranny than that of purely academic theorists, and the pan-Turkish party was of that type. Most offensive of all were the new laws dealing with education. Formerly the Greeks had maintained their own schools on a voluntary basis, and in them instruction was given in their own language. Now the law laid down that there was to be one uniform system of state education throughout the country, and in all schools teaching was to be given in the Turkish language alone, so that the younger generation, whether Greek, Albanian, Armenian, Arab or other would be brought up to speak Turkish. This definite attack upon the nationalities of the near east had much to do with provoking the Balkan War of 1912.

The Young Turks had claimed to set up a constitutional, liberal, and representative government, but when the elections were held it soon became clear that no real freedom of choosing representatives would be permitted, and a preponderating number of Turks was returned, even from provinces where Turks were in a very small minority and unpopular. It cannot be suggested that this or such-like grievances aroused any intense feeling amongst the Turkish or Arab population who had hardly grasped the idea of representative government, but it did seriously affect the loyalty of the Greeks, who are a numerous and commercially important part of the population of European Turkey.

The only justification of a high-handed government would have been striking success in international relations; the Turks had been so long used to losses of territory that a government which prevented further loss or recovered any of the alienated territory could have counted on loyal support. In 1911, however, came the Italian attack on Tripoli, and this was followed by the disastrous Balkan war. The government found that its efforts to force the whole subject population into an Othmanli mould had contributed much to making this war possible. The events of 1911-12 convinced the people of Turkey that the Young Turks were no more likely to restore the prestige of their country than the late Sultan, and were very much more burdensome.

In March, 1912, the " Turk Ojaghi " or " Home of the Turks " was opened at Constantinople, a kind of club and centre of nationalist propaganda, from which all non-Turks were excluded, and which acted as a kind of " power behind the throne " in urging the government to a stricter pro-

Turkish policy, and in accentuating the radical defect of the new règime which we take to be the predominating influence of academic theorists who could not realise the real needs and feelings of the people. The one point in which the pan-Turks were undoubtedly right was in their anti-Slav attitude. The two western powers which seriously threatened Turkey were England and Russia; neither of these could be successfully attacked by any single Muslim power. Abdu l-Hamid's policy of uniting all the Muslim powers in a joint effort—a perfectly sound and reasonable policy—was in abeyance. Of the two Russia was the more threatening; the important territorial losses of 1876 were still fresh in the Turkish mind, Russian policy obviously was aggressive, and was believed to be aiming at Constantinople, and Russian intrigue was behind a great deal of the Balkan unrest. Obviously the wisest plan was to secure some ally who could be relied upon as consistently anti-Russian. In the past Abdu l-Hamid has thus trusted Great Britain, believing that the menace of Russian aggression on India would make the British government sincere in supporting Turkey, and the British had tacitly favoured that by encouraging a fuller recognition of the Khalifate amongst the Muslims of India. But Great Britain did not command absolute confidence; the British occupation of Egypt was disquieting, though everything was done to respect the theoretical claims of the Sultan there; and sometimes the British showed a disposition to resent the treatment of the Armenians in Turkey; but trust in Great Britain did not really come to an end until 1912, when it acted in partnership with Russia in what was practically the partition of Persia. Even under Abdu l-Hamid German policy had striven to increase Turkish suspicion of England, and when it seemed that the western powers were on the point of taking concerted action in dealing with the responsibility of the massacres in Armenia the Kaisar took the opportunity of promising his protection and support if any European powers ventured beyond verbal remonstrance, reaping his immediate reward in the Baghdad railway concession. The Germans were necessarily anti-Russian, and their sincerity in encouraging Turkey and promising support against Russia was beyond question. So far Germany had taken no direct share in the politics of the Muslim world, but it was quite well able to convince Turkey of its military resources and efficiency. The only disquieting point was the German alliance with Austria, the country which seized Bosnia; but even in face of this Turkey was prepared to join hands with Germany, for the anti-Russian policy overrode every other consideration. No doubt the definite alliance of Turkey and Germany was decided when Great Britain openly joined Russia in dealing with Persia. The essential defect in the conditions created by the foreign policy of the Young Turks, as was revealed during the war, was the pan-Turkish dream; it was hoped and expected that all the Turkish races of

Central Asia, including many Russian subjects, would rally round the Sultan, and for the sake of this the leadership of Islam was laid aside, one of the worst instances of giving up the substance for the shadow that history can show. The various Turkish races had no conscious racial unity, and it was very difficult to get them to combine, whilst the pre-war pan-Turkish policy tended to make non-Turkish Muslims very suspicious. The Germans, on their side, over-estimated the spiritual importance of the Khalif, they supposed that he was a kind of Muslim Pope, and that, if he called a holy war, the whole of Islam would rise at once to his call, overlooking the fact that the pan-Turkish movement was undermining the comparatively limited authority conceded to the Khalifate. Since the war, however, the pan-Islamic appeal has been revived, and there has been a growing tendency to regard Turkey as the bulwark against western aggression, and on this ground to rally to her support. The serious danger threatening the Khalifate movement of recent times rises from the Turks themselves lest, if they are left in peace to go their own way, they give rein once more to pan-Turkish ideas, and, in the dream of uniting all the Turkish tribes of Asia, seriously and finally alienate the non-Turkish Muslims in pursuit of an unpractical dream.

The most important nationalist movement outside that of the Turks was that in assertion of Arab nationalism. The racial feud between Turk and Arab is one of long standing. Turkey has never been able to reduce Arabia to a Turkish province, and Turkish control there has always been more or less restricted. As the Turks have become to some extent westernized they have become more and more irritating to the Arabs, who particularly disliked the Turkish officers who came down into the Hijaz with the annual pilgrimage, and regarded them as tinged with atheism, a charge which the Turk of the younger generation often deserves. In 1877, during the ferment produced throughout the Turkish dominions by the disastrous Russian war, this dislike found vent in a wide-spread revolt against Turkish rule, a revolt which was put down in a very ineffectual way, so that large tracts of Arabia were never brought under control at all; in fact, the Turks could do no more than hold the pilgrim route and part of Yemen. Elsewhere, as in Hasa, Turkish rule meant no more than holding a few forts, and occasionally sending out punitive expeditions. If any western power had tried to hold Arabia its experience would have been exactly the same, unless it were prepared to maintain a military force on a vast scale without the prospect of any adequate return. We have recently had an experience of similar sort in 'Iraq, where the task is of the same nature, and a wide-spread feeling has arisen in England that it is not worth continuing.

One method only lay before the Turks as a means of getting a firmer grip on Arabia, namely the construction of strategic railways by means of which troops and material of war could be moved even more rapidly than by camel. The task was not an easy one, for desert railways are difficult to lay and difficult to maintain, and in such a land as Arabia every yard has to be guarded. The ostensible plea for the construction of the Hijaz railway was to ease the pilgrimage, and contributions were invited on religious grounds, though the devout who gave subscriptions very soon had reason to fear that in this, as in every other financial scheme in Turkish hands, speculation and misappropriation were rife. The railway, under the control of German engineers, was hurried down through Syria and Palestine to the borders of Arabia, but here religious difficulties arose. An outcry was made against the presence of unbelievers, and against the penetration of the Muharram, but the railway had already brought Arabia into touch with Syria and Turkey, and the Arabs were well aware of the power this placed in the hands of the Turkish government. Consequently the construction of the Hijaz railway was accompanied by a renewal of what professed to be an Arab nationalist movement, but was really an anti-Turkish agitation, the hope of the Arabs of Arabia being that they would receive the support of the Syrian Arabs, although their grievances were of a totally different character. In Syria the anti-Turkish feeling was mainly due to the fact that the higher ranks of officials were always Turks, and these, of course, had to bear the unpopularity of every error and injustice of the government as well as the feeling natural against foreigners, the jealousy towards those who appropriated to themselves the most lucrative posts, and, no doubt, resentment at the masterful manner of the Turks. Above all, it must be remembered, the Arabs are proverbially hostile toward their rulers, even towards those of their own race, as appears in many passages in the pre-Islamic poets.

The anti-Turkish agitation which passed as a nationalist Arab movement became obvious in 1905, and then for the first time the plea was put forward that the Turks had usurped the Khilafate, that it could only be held by an Arab, and preferably by one of the Quraysh tribe. The evidence of tradition is conflicting; there is a tradition which says that the Khalif must be of the Quraysh so long as there are any of this tribe in existence, and there is another which says that the worthiest Muslim must be chosen as Khalif irrespective of tribe, and this seems most in accordance with the absolute equality and fraternity recorded of the first Muslims; but the whole question is obscure, and good arguments can be brought on either side Admittedly, even when the Arabs were in the minority in Islam, and in some disrepute after the accession of the 'Abbasids, the whole community agreed in recognising an Arab Khalif. We may, however, regard all these arguments as to the theoretical qualifications for the office of Khalif, as well as the claim to a sense of Arab solidarity as ideas brought forward by those who tried to justify and propagate what was really an anti-Turkish agitation,

At the revolution of 1908 the Arabs, taking the proclamations of the "Committee of Union and Progress" at their face value fully hoped and believed that they would now receive recognition of their nationalist claims, that they would be duly represented in Parliament, and share in the privileges of office. But these hopes were soon disappointed. The elections were carefully manipulated, and provision was made that the Turkish representatives should be supreme: the proportion allowed to the non-Turkish races was reduced to the minimum compatible with decency, and only two Arab notables were admitted to the Upper House. Very soon it became clear that the revolution had placed the non-Turkish element in a more marked inferiority than had previously been the case, and that the dominant Turks were striving to eradicate their cherished racial peculiarities, and force them into a Turkish mould. Young Turkish policy thus led to a recrudescence of nationalist agitation in all directions and amongst the resultant movements was that in support of Arab nationalist claims. To a large extent this was a movement of the younger intelligentsia, just as the pan-Turkish movement had been before 1908, and a congress of its adherents was held in Paris in 1913. But before long these theorists got into touch with more practical elements. The centre of the movement was in Syria, and the Syrians succeeded in joining hands with the free Arabs of the desert, and thus formed alliance with the one whom they regarded as their possible champion, the Sharif of Mecca, and he, with his own grievances against the Young Turks, and lured by the ambitious possibilities opened up before him, was quite ready to respond. In this pre-war scheme of the Hijazi kingdom there is much which remains obscured ; it was never more than theoretical and tentative. Egypt had no part in it, for the nationalists there never looked towards the Hijaz ; the Najd, where Ibu Sa'ud was working out his own plans, also lay outside, and in relation to the Wahhabis the Sharif of Mecca was willing to co-operate with the Turks : 'Iraq also was excluded because the Wahhabis lay between : so the pan-Arab movement was in reality a Hijaz-Syria affair only and it is doubtful how far the Syrians then really contemplated Hijazi rule as a matter within practical politics. The Sharif, however, was confident that the formation of an Arab kingdom, under himself *bien entendu*, was feasible, and sent representatives to Cairo, where Lord Kitchener was then the British resident, to find out what would be the attitude of Great Britain in the event of such a thing being attempted. Lord Kitchener received the Sharif's envoy with every courtesy, for the Indian Muslims form a majority of the pilgrims to Mecca, and the Sharif's control of the Holy City made it strongly advisable that he should not take an anti-British attitude, but he informed him that the existing friendship between Great Britain and Turkey absolutely debarred the British Government from any open act in support of the Sharif in the event of his rebellion, and would not facilitate the admission of supplies into Arabia. At the time this was final. Without British support and assistance the projected rising was impossible, so there the matter stood. Arab nationalism remained the academic theory of Syrian litterati who, for the most part, lived outside Syria ; it did not enter the area of practical politics until the war brought changed conditions.

Egyptian nationalist claims were entirely different from either of the two movements we have already considered. It was not a racial claim, for the Egyptians are a mixed race of whom some profess to be Arabs, and amongst whom there is undoubtedly Arab blood, whilst all are Arabic speaking : but the Egyptians did not seek to join the movement in favour of Arab nationalism, and a separate Egyptian nationalism can rest only on the purely western theory of a nation which bases its unity solely upon political community, a theory at first supported by the Young Turks, but afterwards discarded for the racial principle. Like Syria, Egypt was under alien rule, but the alien in this case was British, and professedly Christian, and the nationalist movement was very definitely an anti-English agitation, some at least of the nationalists professing their willingness to be under French rule, many saying that they desired Turkish control, all alike agreeing only in the one perfectly clear opposition to British interference. The Khedivate established by Muhammad 'Ali was practically autonymous when the

British intervened in 1882 in consequence of 'Arabi Pasha's rebellion, and took over control of the country, although the suzerainty of the Sultan of Turkey was still formally recognised. To some extent the conditions resembled those of the native states of India, but were complicated by the theoretical overlordship of the Sultan, and by the peculiar position of the European residents. In theory these Europeans, who were very numerous, were living in a country under Turkish jurisdiction, and so inherited the ex-territorial status secured by "capitulations" made with the Sultan. Very similar conditions prevailed in the middle ages with aliens temporarily resident in any other country, for law was then personal and not territorial, and resident aliens were seldom found unless protected by some treaty made with their natural prince. When the Turks took Constantinople they found colonies of Venetians and Genoese there living under such "capitulations" made by their states with the Byzantine Emperor, and this ancient system survived there, though it became obsolete in the west, because Muslim rulers were not willing to extend their law, largely based on the Qur'an, to embrace Christian aliens, and the Christians were equally unwilling to come under Muslim law, though it must be remembered what the older position was, not that it was a privilege to be exempt from the law prevailing in the community, but that to come under it was a privilege to which aliens were not entitled. So in Egypt each foreign colony was under the jurisdiction of its own consulate, and exempt from the law in force in the native courts, because those courts were theoretically Turkish, Great Britain exercising a kind of " veiled protectorate."

The first act of intervention was necessary to protect the lives of British subjects who were in danger during 'Arabi Pasha's rebellion, and to arrange for the payment of interest and principal of a series of loans made to Egypt which was at the time absolutely bankrupt, and the urgent necessity justified a condition which was anomalous in the extreme, and intended to be only temporary, for it was definitely stated that the British occupation would cease as soon as order was restored and established on a permanent footing, which implied, of course, the ability of the Khedive's government to maintain order. In fact the occupation lasted for more than thirty years, and, it must be admitted, the Egyptian government did not give any very convincing proof of its ability to maintain a permanent and stable control consistent with the safety and welfare of European residents, and of their commercial enterprises. It might be objected that a country does not exist for the benefit of aliens who may be resident; but to this there is the reply that the native government had got into such deep financial difficulties that it had placed itself at the mercy of its creditors, whom it was unable to pay. That it made no proof of efficiency is a fair statement of the way in which the ministers, with few exceptions, pursued their own private ends, and practically made

PAN-ISLAMIC HOPES AND NATIONALISM 143

no effort to meet the obligations of the country, or to secure a stable and effective government. No doubt it may be objected that, under British control they had no opportunity of showing their capacity. Rightly or wrongly the British administrators were of opinion that the country was not ripe for self-government; even if this view were mistaken, it was a judgment formed in perfect good faith by men who were competent observers and admittedly fair-minded. Unfortunately the Oriental tradition of government is vicious, and the British authorities desired to see their own standards of political morality established and regarded the country as unfit for independence until they were. Undoubtedly the maintenance of these standards under British control was deeply appreciated by the fellahin of the generation following the beginning of the occupation; later on the benefits of freedom from capricious exactions, and the establishment of general security, were taken as matters of course, and the rather ungracious manners of those who procured these benefits were more prominent in the minds of observers.

British control continued with the clearly expressed approval of the foreign residents, with one exception, and with the frequently expressed appreciation of the fellahin. During this time the British authorities restored the financial stability of the country, and did very much to improve methods of irrigation, etc., on which the life of Egypt so directly depends. All this meant a considerable outlay in return for which the British shared with other Europeans in the improvements due to restored financial conditions, and held control of the Suez canal which is in an outlying province, which westerns have decided to reckon as a part of Egypt, though no Egyptian has ever regarded the canal area as in other than a foreign, though adjacent, country. It remains for future historians to judge whether the great outlay involved during these years of occupation bears any reasonable relation to the very modest benefits obtained by Great Britain—the benefits to Egypt are undeniable.

How far did the country appreciate these benefits? It is commonly asserted that the fellahin, the vast majority of the population, approved of the British occupation, and this is probably true. Certainly the older men who remembered Turkish rule did so, but generally a newer generation arose which could not remember the old days, and did not appreciate a condition which now seemed to them a matter of course. Still, on the whole, the pre-war fellahin probably were pro-British. Of course there were fanatical Muslims who hated the British simply because they were non-Muslims, and there were particular districts where unfortunate incidents had given the British a bad name. To some extent, no doubt, religious prejudice prevailed in the university of al-Azhar, though possibly not to the extent sometimes believed. Yet there was no definite religious grievance, the changes made by the British were pro-Muslim.

All government offices and schools receiving government grants were compelled to close on Friday, the day of the weekly sermon in the mosque, and no Christian official was allowed to take holiday on Sunday instead : this Sabbatarian observance of the Friday is not usual in Muslim countries, and had not existed prior to the British occupation, it was a novelty devised by the British rulers who inclined to make Islam more puritanical than it had been. Moreover, no one but a Muslim could be Mudir, or governor, of a province, or Omdah or *maire* of a village, or head-master of a state school, although no such sectarian restrictions were imposed under Turkish rule. The Copts, members of the ancient native church, have greatly resented these religious privileges conceded to Muslims by the British ; they seem to have ex- expected that, under Christian influence, they would have themselves enjoyed a privileged position, and even, perhaps, hoped to be able to apply a little pressure to the Muslims, and so they are angry at their disappointment. The Turks, decendants of the ruling class of former days, have held aloof in sulky resentment at being deprived of their privileges. For the most part the anti-British feeling, which has been dignified as nationalism, has flourished in the clerk class, and particularly amongst the post-office employes and the lawyers. With these last we reach an influence which has been steadily keeping sores open and inflaming the sense of grievance, and that is undoubtedly the French interest which has never forgiven the British occupation. Now it must be clearly understood that there is no reason to suspect official French action in this; it has been the attitude of Frenchmen in the country, perpetually striving to embroil France with England, and trying to embarrass the work of English officials in Egypt, really doing their own government no good service by their attitude; but France is a democratic country, and official authority is not always able to suppress intemperate and injudicious supporters. It became the habit for anti-British Egyptians to look to France for encouragement, and this was especially the case with the lawyers as, French and Arabic being the official languages of the courts, they were generally educated under French influences, and often went to France to finish their education, and especially to the university of Lyons, where a special college was established to provide for Egyptian and Turkish students, and where a bitterly anti-British attitude was developed.

The great leader of nationalist aspirations in Egypt was Mustapha Kemal, who died in 1908, and whose " Egyptian-French Letters " still forms the favourite manual of anti-British propaganda, and teaches the young effendi to look to France as the possible liberator from the English yoke. To this expectation the responsible officials of the French Government have given no encouragement, though private deputies have more than once indulged in speeches which have tended to raise nationalist hopes. The Turkish revolution of

1908, the year of Mustapha Kemal's death, produced a wave of excitement in Egypt, and efforts were made to form a Young Egyptian party on similar lines to those followed in the building up of the Young Turks; from this time onwards the nationalists tended to look more towards Turkey. A very strong anti-British animus appears also in the leading poets Hafiz Ibrahim and Shawki Bey, whose great influence as undoubted men of genius has hardly been sufficiently appreciated by British observers.

Great Britain has always claimed that its occupation of Egypt was a temporary measure and, as time went on, the policy of gradual devolution was outlined and begun to be put into practice. Such a policy, corresponding to an orderly retirement in military operations, is an extremely difficult one to carry out successfully; each withdrawal is likely to be regarded as an act of weakness, and the impunity enjoyed by agitators in the exercise of free speech encouraged a vast amount of wildly seditious talk. Very often, also, British officials did make mistakes which gave a handle to agitating demagogues, and the Khedive, 'Abbas Hilmi, seemed disposed to strain the patience of the English advisers to breaking point. At length it became clear that a firm hand was necessary, for Great Britain was not ready for complete evacuation and the attempt to govern through a Khedive who thwarted the British officials at every turn was producing an impossible position and one intolerable for English members of the civil services.

Very prudently Lord Kitchener was put in control and he guided affairs until the outbreak of war in 1914. Although his administration was the most practical and sensible under the circumstances, the anomalous position remained, merely temporarily secured and full of problems for which no solution was as yet proposed.

On the eve of war it was generally believed that the nationalist agitation was confined to the clerkly classes in the towns and that it did not appeal to the fellahin; it was supposed that its adherents formed a small but noisy minority, so small indeed as to be practically negligible. Outside this small class and the Khedive's entourage it was believed that the people at large stood for the British control. As far back as 1903 Meredith Townsend, who knew the East, warned Englishmen that they were generally unpopular in Egypt, and the writings of Hafiz Ibrahim and of many minor poets, who most nearly express the real feelings of an oriental people, emphasized this, whilst admissions to the same effect were made by various English observers who knew the country well. It was widely felt, when war broke out, that a rising in Egypt was to be feared and the probability was viewed with grave anxiety. The only question was, would the revolutionaries get any following amongst the fellahin?— and if the agitation were confined to the effendi class, would it come to more than noisy riots in the leading towns? Even that would be serious enough as there is a distinct vein of hysteria in the Egyptian, dull and slow as he often appears to be, and in a moment of undue excitement he would be capable of all sorts of acts against the little handful of English caught in the midst of a hostile population. But the war made an enormous change. Very soon the country became a huge camp under martial law : during the years of war the population was forced to lie supine and an entirely wrong estimate was formed of the tractibility and pacific character of the people.

India was in a position rather different from that of any of the countries we have considered so far. To begin with, India is a continent and not a country ; a land inhabited by many races at very different stages of social evolution, differing in language, religion and customs. No one of these is entitled to describe itself as Indian to the exclusion of the others, or to claim to know or represent the views and aspirations of the whole. The only kind of union which has ever existed in India has been a temporary co-operation in resisting an invader, and in history such co-operation has been rare, occasional, and local. Here, more than anywhere else, all that claims to be nationalist must be understood as simply anti-European, and usually as anti-British, an intensified feeling against the foreign conqueror, mainly because he is a foreigner, no matter how paternal his autocracy, expressed with that singular freedom which is possible, perhaps, only under the exceptional toleration of British rule. Of this agitation, its motives and tendencies, we have an illuminating exposition in the Mutiny of 1857, all of whose lessons are true for the present time as they were seventy years ago.

In that mutiny the most active agents were the *sipanis* or sepoys, the soldiers employed by the British, and these were the persons who had been especially favoured by the British rulers, not only receiving better pay and pension than any of the soldiers employed by native princes, but enjoying many exceptional privileges. There was no real grievance formulated at the time; the story of men being compelled to taste cows' fat when extracting cartridges, and similar things, were devised later, and were not true. The sole motive was hatred of the alien white ruler, and this hatred was strongest amongst those most in contact with the British, and apparently on perfectly friendly terms with them. At the time all India looked towards Delhi and the living representatives of the house of Timur, the Muslim rulers whom the British had displaced. Even the Hindus, who had fared far worse under the rule of Delhi than under the British, desired to restore Muslim rule. The tolerant and even indulgent European was more intensely hated than the Muslim who had ruled sternly, and certainly inclined to favour his co-religionists. Allowance must be made for the fact that a sufficiently long time had elapsed to dim the recollections of the house of Timur, whose rule had not been very happy in its later period, but the lesson is important that even an Oriental tyrant seemed to many to be preferable to the alien whose whole attitude towards life seemed to far removed from Oriental standards. It is true that the Mutiny was not unanimous, and this, together with the lack of any real leader, made its collapse inevitable. Yet there was, in the ranks of those who mutinied, a representation of very widely divergent racial and religious elements which found a bond of temporary agreement and united action in their dislike of British rule. There is a common tendency to suppose that the peoples of India are so far divided by racial and religious animosities that they never could unite effectively in rebellion against British rule, and considerable surprise has been expressed at their co-operation in the post-war period, a co-operation which many have suspected as unreal: it has been assumed that these internal divisions secure the stability of British authority. It is fairly certain that, if the withdrawal of British control left free play to these rivalries they would rapidly produce a state of civil war: but the Mutiny of 1857 has conclusively proved that anti-British feeling is sufficiently pronounced to permit of their being temporarily laid aside, and that, however friendly feelings may be towards individual British residents, the general feeling is antagonistic. The native mind can never get over the idea that every Englishman is extremely wealthy, and derives part of his wealth from the resources of India. The feeling, however, is negative, it is anti-English, and its leading advocates are especially recruited from those who, having received the dubious benefits of an English education, either find themselves unable to make a living thereby or else consider that their remuneration is inadequate : besides, of course, those who are really animated by religious fanaticism. The weak point invariably has been the lack of adequate leadership. Whether it has been wise policy to allow so great a liberty of speech and agitation to those whose political training has been so widely different from that of the west may be a question : but it is a question of past policy, the attempt to check it now would be doomed to failure.

From time to time, since the Mutiny of 1857, there have been partial risings, or at least local phases of unrest, especially in the North-West. This was the case in the Panjab in 1905, and in 1907 the disaffection there became acute, and a certain number of Afghans and tribes dwelling about the Afghan frontier crossed the border and joined in the disturbances. On the eve of the war there was a wide impression that India was on the verge of another Mutiny, and this seems to have been assumed by German observers, who were confident that the outbreak of war in Europe would precipitate the revolt. Indian life, however, lies very far removed from the currents of European politics, and the outbreak of war in August, 1914, found India rather bewildered and by no means ready to throw itself into the arms of the Central Powers. At that juncture the leading native princes came forward to support the British Government, even those who had previously been showing signs of dissatisfaction, and this, for the moment, was decisive. No doubt the current of generous loyalty was rather helped by the fact that the leading agitators were not, by race or caste, those best calculated to command the attention of the more military races, and were rather regarded with contempt. The general attitude seems to have been that domestic disputes would keep, and it was possible to enter into the war without prejudice to the attitude to be adopted when the war was over.

CHAPTER VII

THE WAR AND AFTER

THE Great War of 1914-1918 has had a very direct bearing on Islam. For some time beforehand the world was prepared by a very extensive propaganda, the more effective because carried out by Germany in perfect good faith, as seems to have been the case. At bottom its spirit may be described as " the Gospel of Efficiency," and this is, in fact, simply the expression in definite form of the peculiar characteristics which have been developed in recent times in western civilization : it is the essence of western culture in its later and more aggressive form. It has been expressed in two ways, as the theory of a state-directed national efficiency, which received its best expression in Germany, and as that of a competitive individualistic efficiency which had its fullest development in the United States of America and in the British colonies. But its essential substance was present in all the western nations, the only difference was that in some there were conservative relics and prejudices which hampered its full growth, whilst in the newer lands this was absent, and the spirit of the times was able to assume full control, and in Germany, though a great deal of the older traditions lingered in the atmosphere of the various states, the Empire itself was free from anything in the way of old-world prejudices and consciously aimed at thoroughness and efficiency in the most modern spirit, and did so with a logical coherency and completeness characteristic of Teutonic mentality. Whether the efficiency desired was or was not the highest form of culture is a question still open for discussion : at any rate in the form presented by Imperial Germany it was to be the full realisation of all those tendencies which had gradually become operative to modern European culture, and undoubtedly the generation of Germans who grew up under the Empire was fully convinced that it was the ideal, and this view was propagated throughout the world with extraordinary energy. The psychology of the group-mind is involved, but in this case the general result was that the whole of the educated community in the west was more or less hypnotized and profoundly impressed by the German claims. Here and there, no doubt, there were recalcitrant elements, a few who were inspired by a love of the older humanities, and a few who were aroused to resentment by the older assertiveness of the missionaries of the new culture, whilst everywhere the main body of the working classes which, in 'te of popular education, still remain out of touch with current tendencies in culture, continued unaffected.

Although the Germans regarded themselves,

L

and were generally regarded, as the foremost exponents of modern civilization, they felt a deep grievance in that they occupied a very minor sphere in the partitioning and development of the lands and the peoples which the west generally regarded as backward ; they considered themselves the best fitted to educate the less progressive races, and the best qualified to exploit their resources. As a matter of fact they did establish colonies in Africa, but found no opening amongst the older Muslim communities, though admittedly German scholars led the world in their knowledge of the religion, history and languages of Islam. It is difficult to estimate the exact range of German contact with the Muslim world : it seems to have been mainly confined to certain sections of the intelligentsia, and its programme was to intensify hatred of the western nations which held political control in Algeria, Persia, Turkey, and India, although the ground of animus in the Germans and the Muslims was diametrically opposed. At the outbreak of war the Germans were confident that Islam would rise *en masse* against the Allies, no doubt over-estimating the importance of the groups with which they had been in contact, whilst the Allies were seriously afraid that such a rising would take place. England, as the most concerned, was at the start most anxious, for it seemed quite likely that the Muslims of India would rise. Whilst the rank and file in this country underestimated the dimensions of the task which the war opened up, the more educated classes in many cases felt confident that it was only a question of time for England and France to go down before the Central Powers, although they were determined to go down fighting. The strong apprehension of defeat deeply felt though nowhere expressed, engendered a certain rashness in making promises; in all probability they would never have to be kept, or if they were to be fulfilled the conditions of the post-war world would be so new that everything was possible; it was a gambling on futurity, and in this spirit promises of self-government and independence were made which afterwards caused serious trouble.

The first outbreak of war found the Muslim countries a little bewildered, the issues involved were so essentially western that the Oriental world failed to find a clue, whilst the Indian army responded readily and without realizing that any problem lay before it. But when, a little later, the Turks threw in their lot with the Central Powers the position was materially changed. This was the first indication that the war in the west had a direct bearing on Muslim interests, and the fact that the Khalif took the side of the Germans produced a very profound impression. In fact Turkey's action was inevitable. The pan-Turanian policy, to which Enver Pasha was deeply attached, took its stand on the idea that Russia was the Turks' chief enemy, and anti-Russian feeling was the one sure guide in Turkish foreign policy. Thus Turkey felt impelled to support the side opposed to Russia, and had already pledged herself to do so in the event of war. As soon as Turkey definitely took sides the Khalif made every effort to declare the war a *jihad*, and called for Muslims to rally round him against the unbelievers. This appeal was singularly unsuccessful. The leading Muslims did not support it: for one thing it was generally felt that the Germans were behind the Sultan, and that the proclamation of the *jihad* was made of the suggestion of non-Muslim advisers, but still more the Young Turk party then in the ascendant at Constantinople, was generally regarded with profound suspicion. Events since 1908 had shown that it was Turkish rather than Muslim, it had succeeded in alienating the Arabic world, and was pictured as atheistic in spirit. The Khalif's appeal in 1914 did not carry the weight which would have gone with a similar appeal from Abdu l-Hamid, who, for all his short-comings, was very truly a Muslim. Yet the call was not without some result. There was a short outbreak of disorder in Egypt, which the British expected and promptly suppressed, and in North-West India, whilst in Tripoli there was a general rising, and the Italians were driven to the coast; but these disturbances were scattered, and without adequate leadership, the more reputable type of Muslim standing aloof for the reasons we have already mentioned, and so they were put down, though not without some difficulty and a considerable feeling of anxiety.

The next event bearing on Muslim interests took place on 25th October, 1915, when the representative of the Sharif of Mecca attended at Cairo and received a definite promise from the representative of the British Government that the Sharif would be formally recognised by Great Britain as Arab king, save in South Mesopotamia and in territory where Great Britain was " not free to act without detriment to the interests of France." In the previous March a secret treaty had been concluded between Great Britain and France, by which French interests were recognised as paramount in Syria in return for a similar recognition of British interests in Egypt. By this the Sharif of Mecca, now referred to as King of the Hijaz, was unexpectedly excluded from Syria, but the secret treaty was not disclosed to the Arabs, and carefully concealed from the British officers who were sent to the Hijaz.

The recognition of the Sharif as King of the Hijaz—the title " King of the Arabs " was claimed by him but never officially conceded by the British authorities—completed the Arab revolt against the Turks. Some time before this the Sharif had been contemplating such a revolt, and had approached Lord Kitchener and asked for support from the British authorities, but it had been definitely refused. Now, in 1915, this was changed, the British themselves made the overtures, and the envoy from Mecca attended in response to the invitation from Cairo. About the same time negotiations were opened with the Sharif's rival, Ibn Sa'ud.

In 1915, and for some time afterwards, the King

of the Hijaz and his Arab followers were fully convinced that the British were pledged to support the formation of a separate Arab kingdom comprising all the Arabic speaking provinces of the Turkish Empire in Asia, with the exception of South Mesopotamia, and had no idea that Syria had been promised to the French. The use of the title " King of the Hijaz," rather than " King of the Arabs," was supposed to be due to a desire not to hurt the feelings of Ibn Sa'ud and of the ruler of Oman, and the Arabs joined in the Palestine and Syrian campaign of 1917 under the impression that they were helping the liberation of the Arab provinces in preparation for the expected kingdom.

It was not until November, 1916, that the Sharif openly revolted against Turkey, and was formally recognised as King of the Hijaz, and thus his revolt followed after the Turkish attack on the Suez Canal and its repulse. Meanwhile another secret treaty—the Sykes-Picot agreement—had been concluded between Great Britain and France in May, 1916, and by this those two powers partitioned the Arab provinces of Turkey outside Arabia definitely French, the Syrian hinterland Arab, but under French "influence," Palestine international but with a British port of Haifa, and all the Arab lands east of Syria and Palestine were to be divided into two " spheres of influence," the one British, the other French.

The support given by the British to the King of the Hijaz opened up momentous questions for the Muslim world. It was generally claimed that the guardianship of the holy cities was one of the prerogatives of the Khalif, some Muslims indeed held that it was the essential feature of a valid Khalifate, whilst it was significant that the Sharif belonged to the tribe of Quraysh to which certain traditions restricted the office of Khalif; and the Sharif described himself in his letters not only as "King of the Arabs" but as "Commander of the Faithful," a title associated with the Khalifate. It seemed, therefore, that Great Britain, for political purposes, had set up an anti-Khalif, and this at once became a burning question. Perhaps it is what had been intended at first, but the earliest indications of the way in which the project was received were so serious that in 1917 very strict orders were enforced in the Indian regiments, forbidding any English officer to discuss the matter in any way or to express any view upon it whatever. It was deeply repugnant to Muslim feeling that a Khalif should be appointed by a non-Muslim power, and used as a political tool by unbelievers, though this feeling did not imply anything like loyalty to the Turkish Sultan. It is true also that there was a prejudice against the Sharif of Mecca in particular, as he and his family were unfavourably known for the exactions which they had long levied upon the pilgrims to Mecca. Perhaps, on the other hand, there had not been any conscious effort to set up a rival Khalif, though the Sharif had private ambitions in that direction. There had been several instances in history where the Khalif for the time being did not really hold the holy cities, sometimes indeed those sacred sites had been in the hands of the Qarmatians or other acknowledged heretics, and in the early nineteenth century the Wahhabis had controlled them, but this fact had never been taken as hindering the validity of the Khalif's title ; moreover canonists were not agreed in the theory that possession of the holy cities conveyed a title to the office of Khalif. However, the question then was, and still is, debated, and it is possible that the apparent use of the Khalifate as a political tool by a Christian power did not counterbalance any help brought by the co-operation of the Arabs.

The King of the Hijaz took the old position that the Young Turks were obviously anti-Arab, that they were indifferent as to Islam, and had profaned the sacred sites in their endeavour to put down the Arabs of Mecca. This is best summarized by the following passage from one of the appeals circulated amongst the tribes, and dropped by aeroplane in the Arab lines of the Turkish forces in Sinai: " The Sultans continued to do well until I made war with the Arabs in the year 1327 to break those who were around Abha, and so to maintain the honour of Turkey. The same contest was repeated in 1328 under the general command of one of my sons, until the Turkish " Union and Progress Committee " appeared and tried to obtain absolute control of the empire, and caused Turkey to take part in the present war, which will be lost, and there will be no more Turkey, as is well known to all. All these doings were for their private ends : they murder, drive into exile, and plunder through the whole country, especially in the sacred territory, compel many of the inhabitants to sell their property and furniture, their doors and roofs, in order to obtain the necessary food. They are not satisfied with all that they have done, but are trying to separate the Muslims of the Turkish Empire from others of the whole world by the way they describe the life of our Prophet Muhammad in a newspaper called " The Diligent," which is published in the metropolis, and this was brought to the notice of the Prime Minister, of the Sheikh ul-Islam, the Ulema, wazirs, and notables. Also they agreed to change the statements of the Qur'an as regards inheritence, and gave equal shares to the son and to the daughter. They abrogated one of the five primary duties of Islam, which is the keeping of Ramadan, as they ordered the troops at Madina and Makka and in Syria not to observe Ramadan, using false arguments which undermine Islam. They limited the power of the Sultan of Turkey to such an extent that he was unable to appoint even his own secretary. Anwar Pasha, Jamal Pasha, and Talaat Bey have turned the government into an absolute despotism. For no reason they hung many of the Muslim notables and learned Arabs, such as the Amir Umar al-Gazayeri, the Amir 'Aref ash-Shahahd, Shafik Bey al-Moyad. . . . .

All these doings were not sufficient to satisfy their selfishness, so they plundered the property of the widows. They have also shown disrespect to the shrine of the Sheikh 'Abd al-Kadir al-Gazayerli. We call to witness the whole human race and Muslims in particular as to the bombardment of the sacred house of God, the Ka'aba, as well as the shrine of Ibrahim, causing many accidents and disasters. Daily they continued to slay three or four men in the sacred house until no one ventured to draw near. We conscientiously could not suffer these things to be done, and deem it necessary to be independent. Our aim is to stand for Muslims and for Islam, and to spread education amongst the Arabs.

"(Signed) AL-HUSSAYN IBN 'ALI
"Sharif and Amir of the Arabs."

In the autumn of 1916, before the Sharif had been publicly proclaimed king, the pilgrimage, omitted in 1915, had gone up from Egypt, the *Mahmal* being conveyed from Suez to Jedda by the *Hardinge* of the Indian navy, and went up to Mecca under British protection. It was very commonly believed, even in Egypt, that British soldiers had proceeded with it to Mecca, but this was not true; no Christian soldiers were allowed to enter the Muharram, though British aeroplanes flew over the pilgrims and around Mecca itself. Outside Hijazi circles, however, this Christian intervention in the most sacred rites of the religion of Islam was looked at askance, and allowance was not made for the fact that without some such intervention, which was used most cautiously, the pilgrimage would have been impossible: the impression, nevertheless, was that Islam had fallen into the hands of the British. But many recognised that conditions were abnormal, and that in the preceding year the pilgrimage had to be omitted altogether. The Muslims of the Indian army remained loyal, but the non-Arab Muslim world seems to have set itself from the very first definitely against the King of the Hijaz who was considered to have sold the prestige of Islam for his own private ambition.

The war came to an end in 1918, and very soon afterwards French troops began to occupy Syria. A French force, which called itself " the Syrian Expedition," had already operated in Palestine under General Allenby, and seems to have taken for granted that Syria when conquered would be handed over to the French, but the British public had no knowledge of the secret treaty which was, of course, entirely unsuspected by the Arabs. The occupation of Syria by the French was a disagreeable surprise, as the Arabs who had been serving in the campaign, and those in Syria had quite looked forward to independence, and they now began to show signs of dissatisfaction. It was felt, however, that there was some misunderstanding, which would soon be put right, and the Emir Feisal, son of the King of the Hijaz, persuaded the Arabs to entrust the matter to him as their spokesman, and this they did, for the

Emir had won their confidence by his good leadership of the Arab forces during the invasion of Palestine. Thus appointed as the representative of the Arabs, he attended the Peace Conference at Versailles, which produced the treaty of June, 1919, and then for the first time the secret treaties between Great Britain and France were disclosed. The disclosure was followed by an outburst of popular indignation in France; it was said that the country had been duped, that it was generally understood that all Syria was to be French and not merely a strip of coast, and the press declared that England had been the deceiver, securing the whole of Egypt for herself, and cheating France out of Syria. Before this storm the French Government quailed, and opened up new negotiations with England, whilst the Emir Feisal went over to London to urge the fulfilment of the promises made to the Arabs in 1916. His efforts, however, were of no avail: the terms of the Sykes-Picot agreement were read in the strictest sense, so that the French " sphere of influence " inland became practically a protectorate, and the French determined to press this to the fullest possible extent. During the whole of 1919 the Allies were inactive, because occupied with their private disputes, chiefly due to the antagonism aroused in France in the Chamber, in the press, and in the country at large, and the first decisive step was taken by the Arabs who held a pan-Syrian congress early in 1920, and formally elected Feisal King of Syria, thus claiming the right of self-determination which President Wilson had declared to be one of the objects of the war. It is not easy to follow the state of opinion in Syria; there are various communities, different in race and creed, and certainly these would not normally agree in their desires: some of them favoured an Arab kingdom, some did not; of those who did some were willing to accept the Emir Feisal, others did not desire a comparative stranger as ruler. Even in Damascus itself Feisal did not receive unquestioning support, and it was uncertain how far he could count on the loyalty of his subjects, save under one condition, namely, their co-operation in opposing a foreign invader. There were, however, some, notably the Maronites, who called for French intervention, regarding the Arabs as foreigners as much as the French, and of the two the less desirable.

The French regarded the formation of the Arab kingdom of Syria as a direct challenge, as indeed it was; even if the Syrian hinterland were no more than a French "sphere of influence" the establishment of a state there without their consent, and with the declared purpose of excluding their control, was provocative. The persons who felt most aggrieved, however, were the Arabs of the coast area, who found themselves kept out of the Arab kingdom, and relegated to the position of French subjects; they had participated in the Congress at Damascus, and now claimed the right of self-determination, so that they might join King Feisal. So far the coast Arabs had been disposed of to France without their opinion or consent being asked, and thus in violation of the much advertised principles laid down by President Wilson ; they now claimed to express their views, and emphasized the claim by riots at Beirut and other coast towns. Unfortunately this played into the hands of the French authorities, for they were technically French subjects, and the riots justified military measures for restoring order. Alarmed at the events in Syria, and the disturbances which were taking place about the same time in Mesopotamia, the Premiers of the Allies met at San Remo, and drew up terms based on the Sykes-Picot agreement, which was now put forward as a " mandate " under the newly-formed League of Nations, and then a British force was sent out to Mesopotamia, a French force to Syria, and a mixed force of British, French, and Greeks to Constantinople.

The French contingent of nearly 100,000 men, under command of General Gouraud, an experienced colonial officer, landed in Syria on July 13th, and the commander at once sent up an ultimatum to the Emir Feisal, which the Emir accepted. This, however, was ignored, and a force of 60,000 men was sent up to Damascus to depose him. The Emir was too prudent to attempt direct resistance, and retired to the desert fighting a rearguard action as he went. On July 25th the French entered Damascus, and occupied the city, imposing a fine of 10,000,000 francs for its " rebellion," and imprisoning and executing several of the nationalist leaders : the whole country was reduced to the condition of a French dependency, and was handled somewhat severely by General Gouraud.

Meanwhile Mesopotamia had been occupied by the British, and organised more or less as a British colony, Egypt was a British protectorate, and Palestine was being made a Jewish colony under British control. It was obvious that the Allies were determined to partition all the Arab provinces of the Turkish Empire outside Arabia, and thus European aggression took a more formidable aspect than ever in the past.

The events of 1919-1920 in themselves warned the Muslim world that it was in imminent danger of servitude to Europe, or at least to the victorious Allies, and in the desperation produced by the nearness of the peril, scattered risings took place in various parts, at first rather futile because lacking in co-operation and leadership. Already, however, two powers were appearing on the horizon which promised to change this condition and to help the world of Islam to resist the advance from the west. These two were Bolshevik Russia and Kemalist Turkey.

The revolution of 1917 completely changed the political position of Russia and its relation to the other powers of Europe. It is quite unnecessary here to recapitulate the several changes which took place there between the revolution and the Armistice, as the Muslim world was directly affected only by the Bolshevik government, which was established at Moscow in November, 1917, and in the course of the same month, by an almost bloodless revolution, set up a Soviet or advisory council at Tashkend in Turkistan. Before the revolution, in 1916, Germany had tried to influence Central Asia and to arouse Turkistan against Russia and Afghanistan, and India against Great Britain—indeed, the formation of a definite Central Asian policy in 1916 was a move which had already caused serious anxiety in Russia and Britain and was a logical development of the pan-Turanian policy then dominant in Turkey. The German agents had, of course, free circulation as far as the Turkish frontier. To the east of that frontier lay Persia, nominally neutral and recently brought under the "influence" of Russia and Great Britain. But Persia chafed greatly under this tutelage and did not preserve her neutrality. To a large extent this was due to the free use of German gold, but at the same time it must be remembered that the attitude of Persia towards Russia was very much the same as that of Turkey, and for the same reasons. As early as 1915 the Germans had managed to sweep away the scattered British colonists—consuls, bankers, and telegraph officials—in Central and South Persia, and it was well known in 1916 that the country, though professedly neutral, was a centre of German activities and that there were many German and Turkish agents passing across into Afghanistan and Turkistan. To check this a cordon of British and Russian troops was formed and extended from Kuh-i-Malik-i-Sia, where the British frontier touches Persia and Afghanistan, to Transcaspia, a distance of some 600 miles. The Russian revolution of March, 1917, and the formation of a Bolshevik government in the following November meant the breaking of this cordon and the collapse of the effort to exclude German agents, and early in 1918 a corps of Germans and Turks was on its way to Baku and German instructors appeared in Turkistan and Afghanistan. But an even more serious result followed immediately from the Russian revolution. In Russian Turkistan there were some 200,000 Austrian prisoners, largely Magyars by race. The revolution set these free and many of them went south to Afghanistan, and thus it came to pass that very often the forces with which the British had to deal in Central Asia were led by Austrian officers.

Already towards the end of 1917 the Bolshevik government formulated an oriental policy, or rather adapted to itself the existing oriental organizations of the Tsarist régime. Indeed, under Bolshevik rule Russia seems to have become much more of an Asiatic and less of a European power than formerly: perhaps it never was so European as it claimed to be. The key note of the Bolshevik Asiatic policy undoubtedly was the effort to embarrass the western powers by creating difficulties in the east, for it was recognised that the "Capitalist" states of the west were the determined foes of communist Russia. Throughout we note two stages in Bolshevik policy both at home and abroad : at first there was a kind of idealism under which it was supposed that everyone who saw the admirable qualities of communism would at once embrace it and it was only necessary to clear out of the way those reactionaries who were deliberately trying to put obstacles in the way : but this was of short duration, for it very soon became evident that the Russian peasantry would have nothing to do with communism, and the vast majority of the people were against it ; but its advocates were not discouraged—the people were too ignorant to recognise their own true interests and must be educated, by force if necessary, until they did : thus communism entirely discarded the will of the people and took the same attitude as the benevolent despots of an earlier age. The same changes happened in Asia. At first Russia encouraged the formation of independent republics in west and central Asia, but gradually these were all brought into line by means of a series of treaties of alliance until Moscow stood at the head of a nominal federation over which it had the same autocratic control which the Tsar claimed over the Empire, but carried out its control far more drastically and tyrannically. The earlier stage was marked by the peaceable formation of a Soviet at Tashkend in November, 1917 : but a new stage was reached when Bolshevism was extended to Kokhand in the following February, and 10,000 Muslim inhabitants murdered after the city was taken. By 1919 the professed policy of the Bolsheviki was to use force because those who had been brought up under the capitalist régime could not voluntarily adapt themselves to the new conditions: the only hope of communism lay in the younger generation, and the Bolsheviki have made steady efforts to use education for the furtherance of their principles; meanwhile communism is only marking time and clearing the ground for the real work of the future. For the terrible disorders which have followed the revolution, the famines, epidemics, and destruction of life and property, so far as these have been due to human agency the blame seems about equally due to the Bolsheviks and their opponents, in neither case, perhaps, to the leaders, but the civil disorder has released a primitive barbarism which has plunged the whole country back in its social progress. And, besides these human agencies, it must be remembered that the war was followed by the worst season of drought which Russia has experienced for many years. All the troubles through which Russia itself has passed have been reproduced, sometimes in a worse form, in its Asiatic dependents. The history of Bolshevik rule in Ashkabad shows a series of successive reigns of terror, and very similar conditions seem to have prevailed in the other soviet republics: perhaps the tyranny of Moscow became necessary at last as the only salvation from anarchy.

In their Asiatic policy the Bolsheviki were repeating the tactics of the Central Powers who had tried to utilize the east to divert the Allies from putting their whole strength upon the western front. The plans for carrying out the Bolshevik policy were more fully developed in 1918 when three departments were established to investigate and conduct operations: one of these was to deal with the Muslim countries, the second with India, and the third with the Far East. The Asiatic department of the Russian foreign office and its director, M. Alexis Koznessensky, was retained, whilst many of the agents who had worked for the Germans and Turks were employed. The old Lazarev Institute of Oriental Languages at Moscow was continued, though the name " Lazarev " was dropped, and later on was founded the " Scientific Association of Russian Orientalists " with a special periodical the *Novy Vostok* " the New East," edited by M. Pavlovitch (Weltmann). We must admit that the Moscow Soviet has surpassed every other government in its use of journalism as a means of propaganda, and this applies to its Asiatic policy as well as its other activities. But, from 1920 and to some extent even before that date, the serious attention of Bolshevism has been concentrated on the younger generation: it is felt that the adult population is hopeless and is only spared, under strict régime, until the next generation is ready. It is, perhaps, hardly recognised in the west how little any concession to " capitalism " at the present means to the Bolshevik; it is simply a temporary expedient during the period of marking time; Bolshevism proper is to begin when the next genera-

THE WAR AND AFTER

tion is ready. Great importance, therefore, is attached to the education of the young in communist principles, and this particularly applies to the Asiatic races who are invited to send representatives to the " Communist University of Workers in the East " where, in the summer of 1922, there were 700 students. Another 300 were under instruction in the branch university at Tashkend, where there is a special school for women attended by about 50. These institutions, it must be understood, are not universities in the ordinary sense, but simply seminaries devoted to training communist missionaries. In addition the Bolshevik authorities have shown exceptional activity in promoting education generally, in founding village schools, and in schools for adults. They seem to be perfectly sincere in their conviction that their principles are not appreciated simply because of the prejudices instilled by the influences of the old régime and their serious efforts are directed towards securing the coming generation.

As the Bolshevik movement spread out into Asia it had for some time to meet the opposition of the Menshevik armies as well as of the remnants of the old Imperial regiments which still remained loyal, and other hostile elements, especially in Bokhara and Russian Turkestan. The Tashkend Soviet, established in 1917, was cut off from Moscow by a loyalist army of Orenburg Cossacks in the steppes towards the Sea of Aral, whilst another Cossack force held the area between the Sea of Aral and the Caspian. Besides these armies the Bolsheviki met with resistance on the Mongolian frontier, in the valley of Ferghana, and on the steppes to the east of the Caspian, from various local elements strengthened by a certain proportion of officers and N.C.O's of the old Imperial army. On the Bolshevik side the main strength seems to have been the Magyar and Austrian ex-prisoners of war, whilst efforts were made to rouse the fighting tribes of Turkistan and North Persia. The Bolsheviks were masters of the Caucasus in the course of 1918 and aimed at union with Persia and the nationalist leader Kuchik Khan, who was at the head of a body of *Jungalis* or "forest men," assisted by German and Turkish officers and held a large part of the south shore of the Caspian. The regiments raised from the ex-convicts in Siberia were not a success and the chief of these, the Zhlobinskis, were cut to pieces by the Panjabis at Kaakha.

Both on the side of the Bolsheviki and on that of the British, Afghanistan was regarded as of primary importance. At the time the Afghan ruler was the Amir Habibullah who was definitely and steadily pro-British in his policy. In 1906 he had founded the Habibiyah College for boys in which western studies such as English, mathematics, and geography were taught by graduates of Lahore University, and in the following year he had made a visit to India and met the Viceroy at Agra. But Habibullah's pro-British attitude did not meet with universal approval and there was a strong opposition headed by the Amir's brother, Nasarullah. In the border troubles of 1908, large numbers of

Afghans crossed over into India to fight against the
the English and the enterprise was widely preached
as a *jihad*, with the tacit approval of Nasurullah and
the open support of Nazir Safir Khan, the Amir's
seal-bearer and head of police. The Amir, however,
took a very firm attitude and threatened to punish
anyone found preaching a *jihad* against the English
whilst Nazir Safir Khan was blown from the mouth
of a cannon for supplying rifles to those who
went down to take part. But besides the
reactionary element, animated by dislike of English
influence and by the preaching of the mawlawis ag
against the evils of intercourse with unbelievers,
there were the independent Pathan tribes about the
border who have never submitted to the Amir and
who, at all times, have been most dangerous to the
North-west frontier. It was they alone who had
attacked India in 1897, and it was only the pro-
British attitude of the Afghan Amir in their rear
which restrained them in 1908. In the Great War
the Amir continued his steady friendship for the
British in spite of the activity of German agents
who found inflammable material in the anti-British
opposition. In 1918 the Bolsheviki feared Afghanistan as a power likely to make an invasion of Turk-
tan, whilst the British, aware of the divergent
elements there, were also regarding it with mis-
givings. At the time, however, there was a good
deal of uncertainty about the policy and prospects
of the Bolsheviki in Asia and missions were sent,
partly to assist the Persians whose country seemed
to be threatened, and partly to investigate, one in

the west under Major General Dunsterville, whose special task was to organise Baku against a possible Turkish attack, another in North-East Persia under Sir Wilfred Malleson, and a third through Kashgar to Tashkend under Sir George Macartney.

Early in 1919, the Amir Habibullah was murdered and his third son, Amanullah, a vehement enemy of the British, was placed on the throne. There is no reason to impute the murder to Bolshevik agency, though it suited them very well, and happened most opportunely when they were just beginning their propaganda across the frontier. The new Amir, like many of his fellow-countrymen, had chafed at the forced inactivity which had prevented Afghanistan from availing itself of the golden opportunities offered by the years of war and, as we know, had several times entered into negotiations with Turkish and German agents, though without much result so long as his father was alive.

At the time of Habibullah's assassination the Bolshevik agents were employed in active propaganda across the frontier. In the course of 1919 certainly they were active in North-West India and were directly involved in the rioting and scattered outbreaks which occurred with great frequency all through that year and spread over the greater part of the northern provinces.

The Bolshevik agents took the obvious course of encouraging the Nationalist movements which were already in existence, but which, so far, had been somewhat aimless and lacking in co-operation. The Nationalist agitators had been active talkers, but had not produced many men of action or of capacity for leadership, nor had they appealed much to the fighting races who generally tended to regard the rhetorical babu with contempt. Now, however, they found themselves in touch with a large and well-organised system which was ready to direct their energies into more promising channels and to enable them to find a more effective outlet for their aggrieved feelings. Theoretically it would seem that the Bolshevik champions of internationalism must have been guilty of exceptional hypocrisy in lending themselves to nationalist agitations. No doubt they were quite willing to do so simply as a *ruse de guerre*, but it does not seem that it was simply a pretence. They regarded Great Britain as the leading " capitalist " power, seeking to introduce nationalism into Asia, and nationalist movements seemed to them as largely inspired by antagonism to this hated system. Whether the words we have cited already (cf. p. 87 supr.) as placed by the *Izvestia* on the lips of the Amir's envoy to Moscow were really used by him or not, they undoubtedly express the Bolshevik view and the opinions which Bolshevik agents promulgated in Asia, and to a certain extent, they present a logical attitude. The Bolsheviki were correct in diagnosing capitalist enterprise as the aspect of western civilization which was most menacing to Asia, for it was the " concessions " made to commercial undertakings which had done most to interfere with the social and economic conditions prevailing there. As yet the Communist antidote to capitalism was not to the fore-front, and until positive Communism and the class war were emphasized, which was not done by the Bolshevik agents in Asia until 1920, common action could be taken in perfect good faith.

In the earlier phase of Bolshevik activity when the leaders were anxious to obtain the support of the Asiatic races every encouragement was given to the formation of local independent republics, indeed this seems to have been the chief change of policy from that of the Provisional Government which in a proclamation of 9th April, 1917, had definitely refused to recognise the right of self-determination on the part of local and racial groups. After the Bolshevik *coup d'etat* several such independent republics were formed, their number amounted to 32 in the course of the next few years, and of these fourteen were predominantly Muslim, chief amongst them the Republic of Azerbaijan (Transcaucasia) which claims the title " First Muslim Republic." For mutual defence these were invited to federate with Russia which some of them did, and a special office was formed at Moscow to deal with these confederate states under the name of " Commission of Nationalities." By a decree of 16th December, 1920 (cf. *Izvestia* of 21 : 12 : 20) agents from this Commission had to attend every meeting of the representative bodies of each federated republic, with the right of speaking and voting, and was charged to report all proceedings to Moscow and to notify the members of the policy considered expedient by the Moscow Soviet. These agents were sent to all the various states, and those which had not voluntarily made treaties of alliance with Moscow were pressed to do so. Gradually the reins were drawn tighter and by the new constitution formulated at the Tenth Communist Congress held at Moscow, in March, 1921, followed by the decree of 27th July, 1922, these republics became no more than provincial departments under the Moscow government.

At an early stage of this evolution the Moscow Soviet definitely adopted the policy of recognizing regional divisions, but refusing recognition to racial or religious groups non-territorial in character: thus the *Red Soldier* of 18 : 2 : 21, states that the Soviet " thoroughly favours the desire of the people to possess regional autonomy. By regional autonomy the Soviets intend to grant the right to autonomy to the community of workers of a region, province, or country irrespective of their nationality. It cannot therefore contemplate the proposal of granting autonomy to one nationality to the detriment of another. The power of the Soviets cannot favour any national movement in such forms as are manifested in the Ukraine, in the Tartar Republic, etc. These essentially bourgeois forms have no other object than to reduce the native working classes to servitude." (Cited, J. Castagne : *Le Bolchevisme et l'Islam*, Paris, 1922, pp. 14-15.) The separation of Church and State has involved the confiscation of all the *wakfs* or religious trusts recognised by Muslim law and this has aroused the strongest resentment amongst the orthodox of Islam. Sapharov, in a report presented to the

Tenth Communist Congress declared that it is the intention of the Soviet to put down the *Shariat* or canon law of the muslims which he describes as a survival from a past age, " the ishans, mullahs, ulema, form a class of leisured and cultured persons who exploit the people by the help of their historical traditions and religious beliefs." (Cf. Castagne, *op. cit.*, p. 37.) The Bolshevik State has declared itself opposed to Islam as well as to other religious bodies.

In March, 1918, a Bolshevik Soviet was established at Baku where there were many workers connected with the oil industry and of these a large number were Russians. In the following July this Soviet fell before the army of the Azerbaijan Republic which held all the Caucasus district south of Baku, and was definitely anti-Bolshevik in policy. As soon as the Republic captured the city it made it the capital of Azerbaijan and it so remained until April, 1920, when the Russian army, having definitely put down Denikin's movement, advanced on Baku. The Republican Army was then engaged in war with Georgia and the Bolshevik advance practically met with no resistance ; indeed these fatal racial and national quarrels were the real cause of the loss of independence in all the local republics, either they were too much occupied in these disputes to resist the advance of the Bolsheviks or else Moscow made temporary alliance with one of the disputants and got control, after which resistance was too late. The desire of the Bolsheviki was to spread into Persia, but their attitude toward British interests in Asia was not then clearly understood. The Tsarist generals Bisherakoff and Baratof declared for the Allies and sold their services to Great Britain at a somewhat inflated figure. The part of Persia nearest the Caspian, between Manjil and the sea, was held by Kuchik Khan and his Jangalis. Thus matters stood when the Armistice was declared in November, 1918. After that the position was somewhat simplified as it became clear that the Bolsheviki intended to continue war against the Allies and Russia was excluded from the Armistice. In the course of the winter of 1918-1919, the Bolshevik government began to take more active measures to stir up the Muslim world against the Allies and founded the " League for the Liberation of Islam." About the same time they began to encourage the formation of independent Soviet Republics in Azerbaijan, amongst the Tartars of Kazan, the Bashkirs, the Kirghiz and others ; not all these were afterwards suffered to continue but, as expedient, were absorbed in Bolshevik Russia. For the time, however, the Bolsheviki gained the favourable opinion of the Muslim world by renouncing all the concessions which Russia had formerly held in Persia and elsewhere. In Persia Great Britain and Russia had both invested capital, but that invested by Russia had been borrowed from Great Britain, so that the renunciation was very much an act of generosity with other people's money, so far as the Bolsheviki were concerned. In the eyes of the Muslim world, however, this all appeared a generous and unselfish policy and Russia was able to pose as the champion of the downtrodden races of Islam. Such championship was the more readily seized as the Western powers at the Peace Conference showed themselves by no means disposed to lay aside their predatory attitude, indeed they revealed themselves to the world as even more aggressive than before and determined to partition whatever remained of the Turkish Empire, the only remaining Muslim state of any considerable size. This determination to share Turkey amongst themselves put the Allies in the light of tyrants of unbounded rapacity, and the whole Muslim world shuddered with very real fear, for it seemed as though the war had left the allies in the position of over-powering superiority and Islam lay helpless at their mercy. And not only had the Allies disposed of the territorial possessions of Turkey, but one of them, Great Britain, had apparently seized the supreme office of Khalif and disposed of it to one of its creatures. This was not, perhaps, strictly accurate, but it was the way in which Islam generally regarded the state of affairs. Under these circumstances it is not surprising that Muslims looked with some hope towards the one power which still remained at war with the Allies and seemed able to hold its own, a power which was vigorously proclaiming its friendship for Islam and had given proof of its good faith by the formal renunciation of those concessions to which it had a reasonable claim. The economic theories of the Bolsheviki did not receive any great attention ; they dealt with conditions which hardly lay within the practical experience of Asia and of which a plausible explanation could be given to inconvenient enquirers.

Towards the end of 1919, a general congress of Muslims was held in Berlin under Talaat Pasha and this was attended by representatives of the Moscow " League for the Liberation of Islam." The President carried great weight and he definitely advised the Muslims of Asia to join with the Bolsheviki, advice which finally brought over such Central Asiatic Muslims as were still wavering. Not long after this the Bolsheviki occupied Baku. Early in the the following year (1920), however, they experienced a serious check in Persia. It became practically impossible to get any spies across the frontier and, as the Bolsheviki were now trying to deal with Armenia which blocked the way between them and the Kemalist Turks, they were unable to spare the forces necessary for a serious invasion of Persia At this juncture they appealed to Khuda Verdi Sardar, a Khurasan brigand who professed to be a Persian nationalist, and sent him 100 magazine rifles and some machine guns. Thus helped, Khuda Verdi Sardar took Krasnovodok and prepared to invade Persia, but was diverted to Khushk and his rising finally suppressed by the Panjabi forces acting under the Indian government.

The non-success of this effort caused considerable annoyance to the Bolsheviki, and in April, 1920, a conference of Muslim representatives was held in the Foreign Office at Moscow, chiefly memorable for the attendance of Prof. Barrakalula and other

Indian delegates who endeavoured to make plans for a general rising in India. Emissaries were sent from this conference to Afghanistan to secure the co-operation of the new Amir and prevent the Afghans from giving further help to the British authorities in India, and it was decided to invade Khurasan. Not long after this complaints were received from the Soviet in Tashkend stating that Bokhara was a serious obstacle to Bolshevik progress. It was decided therefore to sweep Bokhara aside. The Amir of Bokhara understood the menace hanging over him and sent a piteous appeal with a copy of the Qur'an to the Amir of Afghanistan, his fellow Muslim, but to no avail. Bokhara was attacked, sacked, and reduced. By July, at latest, the Bolshevik emissaries to Afghanistan had been successful and Moscow was finally delivered from any fear of Afghan opposition.

In September, 1920, an Oriental Congress was held at Baku in order to strengthen the union of Muslims and others against the Allies, but at this congress the Bolsheviki over-reached themselves. They judged, erroneously, that the time had now arrived to disclose the full Communist programme to the people of Asia, and to arouse them, not only against the capitalists of the West, but against those of their own number to whom the term " capitalist " might be applicable, the wealthy landowners and tribal chieftains who were the persons primarily responsible for selling the concessions to western speculators. But the world of Islam had none of the class consciousness developed in the industrial communities of the West; the declaration of the "class war" presented Bolshevism in an odious attitude and from this moment there was a distinct drawing back of the responsible leaders of Islam from the Bolshevik alliance. Bolshevik agents continued to operate in 'Iraq, Persia, where an official representative of the Moscow Soviet was formally received early in 1921, Afghanistan, and India, and Muslims were quite ready to avail themselves of Russian help in contending with the western powers, but the disclosure of the Bolshevik programme made at Baku disposed the leaders to caution, to a distinct tendency to disown the extremer agitators who advocated unqualified union with Moscow, and to an inclination to withdraw from an alliance so subversive of the religious principles of Islam, as becomes apparent from this date. Perhaps the candid attitude of the Bolsheviki towards Islam has since been modified; that would be quite in accordance with the present Bolshevik policy of postponing their Communist aspirations until the next generation, educated in these principles, is ready to take up the task. Certainly the similar candour towards Hindus, which also dates from the Baku Conference, has been modified by the circular of 25:11:22 issued to Bolshevik agents in India, which admits that it is now perceived that Hindus are not ripe for Communism, and that the Moscow Soviet was mistaken in supposing that they were, so that advocacy of Communism must be laid aside for the present (Cited, *Times*, 1st January, 1923, p. 9.) Apparently September, 1920, represents the high-water-mark of Bolshevik influence in Islam, and we may consider that from that date it has ceased to receive the same ready recognition as before and that the responsible leaders of Islam are no longer likely to be led blindly by the Bolsheviki, although they may co-operate where they suppose that they are able to do so without coming under Bolshevik influence, though their own estimate of their ability to keep free may be mistaken. The Baku Conference showed that the description of the disintegrating tendency of Bolshevism was not a mere libel, as had been supposed, but pictured a very real danger.

The second new factor of primary importance was the rise of a new Turkish state under Mustapha Kemal. This leader had distinguished himself during the war, but in 1917, convinced that the Allies would ultimately win, he advocated a separate peace. This proposal was rejected and the Turks continued fighting until 1918, when their defence was broken down as he had foreseen. It was fully recognised that Turkey was defeated, and the Turks were prepared to submit to any terms proposed, though assurances were given that Constantinople would not be taken away from them. The one hopeful side was the collapse of Russia in 1917, and the consequent deliverance from what had been the most formidable menace. The Peace Conference of 1919, however, brought a very dreadful revelation. It was clear that the Allies were even more rapacious and selfish than had been suspected before the war, and they seemed determined to break up Turkey and share its provinces between themselves. At that time the Allies were intoxicated by success and acted as though they could deal with the world just as they wished.

In the partition made France received Cilicia, and Greece, an old enemy, particularly obnoxious to the Turks, was encouraged to establish an Empire which would include a large part of Asia Minor. The Turks, however, in spite of long mis-government and inefficient rulers, are not an exhausted and feeble race and were by no means inclined to submit tamely to the proposed dismemberment. Resentment and a determination to resist were most readily felt in Anatolia, the old settlement of the Saljuq Turks of which Koniyeh is the capital, and the Anatolians found their leader in Mustapha Kemal. In August, 1919, under his presidency, a conference was held at Erzerum at which a protest was made at the proposed dismemberment of Anatolia and Thrace. In the following month a second conference was held, this time at Sivas, and similar resolutions of protest were passed. The Anatolians were still under the impression that the Allies intended to adhere to the pledges given before the Armistice by President Wilson and others, securing to each country the right of self-determination so that no country should be disposed of in a way contrary to the expressed wishes of the inhabitants. But the resolutions passed at Erzerum and Sivas were totally ignored. Mustapha Kemal and his adherents now perceived that there was nothing to hope from the Allies and looked round for any other possible support. In one quarter only did they perceive the ability and willingness to help them —in Russia which professed to have renounced all Imperialistic ambitions, and had declared war against the grasping policy of the West. Towards the end of 1919, the "National Council" of the Turks in Asia Minor, led by Kemal, decided to enter into an alliance with the Bolsheviks. About the same time the Bolsheviks got hold of Baku, and only Armenia in the way prevented the actual junction of the Bolsheviks and Kemalists, and upon Armenia now fell the attack from either side.

On January 28th, 1920, the National Council of Asiatic Turks made the "National Pact" by which they pledged themselves to maintain the resolutions passed at the conference at Sivas, and Mustapha Kemal began raising a volunteer army to oppose the carrying out of the Allies' proposals. His action was enthusiastically supported by many of the deputies in the Parliament at Constantinople. But in March the Allies seized those Nationalist deputies and deported them to Malta. In Asia Minor the Kemalists held their course, and on the 29th April, a Nationalist Parliament was assembled at Angora, which from that time forward began to be regarded as the capital of the independent Turkish State in Asia Minor. This, following closely after the Amir Feisal's *coup d'etat* in Syria, somewhat alarmed the Allies, though they do not seem yet to have regarded the Kemalist movement as more than one of the disturbances, more or less endemic in Asia Minor. In the " Supreme Council " held at San Remo it was decided that, whilst Mesopotamia should go to Great Britain and Syria to France, East Thrace, Smyrna, and the Kaza of Aivali should be assigned to the Greeks, East Anatolia to the Armenians, the rest of Anatolia to be divided into " zones," one under French influence, the other Italian, whilst a combined force of British, French, and Greeks were to occupy Constantinople. From this last the Italians were left out because the Premier, Signor Nitti, declined to take part in the proposed partition, foreseeing that it would involve a difficult and costly war. The Greeks by this arrangement received a great deal more than their actual share in the war seemed to justify, but M. Venizelos, the leader of the Imperialistic party in Greece, undertook to provide an adequate force to operate in Asia Minor, and to put down the Kemalists, an undertaking upon which neither Great Britain nor France was at the moment desirous of embarking, as in both those countries voices were heard calling for retrenchment and opposing new military schemes.

In July, 1920, the British, French, and Greeks occupied Constantinople, and forced the Sultan to declare Mustapha Kemal a rebel. They then compelled the Turkish government to send representatives to Sèvres where, on August 10th, they affixed their signatures to the treaty. Although these representatives were mere creatures of the Allies and signed merely as they were ordered, the government at Constantinople ventured on a formal protest when the terms of the treaty were officially communicated. Of course, the Nationalist government at Angora was not consulted, as it had been declared a rebel body. By this time the French and British had to encounter formidable difficulties in Syria and 'Iraq respectively, and this made them take a rather more modest view of the respect and authority which they could command. The Angora government now was left to be dealt with by the Greeks, and they immediately sent an expedition to Asia Minor, and at first made some progress : as yet the Kemalist forces were no more than an irregular volunteer body and in a somewhat experimental stage and held themselves inland in the mountainous country, so that the Greeks were able to overrun and control the more fertile and populous seaboard. When the invaders attempted to penetrate further inland they found themselves faced by many difficulties, and by this time the Kemalist army was beginning to take shape, and was no longer one to be despised.

In February, 1921, a conference was held in London at which the allied powers of Great Britain, France, Italy, Japan, and Greece were represented and which was attended also by envoys from Constantinople and Angora, the latter now for the first time obtaining formal recognition as a sovereign state. At this conference it was proposed to appoint a Commission to deal with the question of Turkey, and more particularly with the partition of Asia Minor, both parties to abide by the finding of the Commission and the rest of the Treaty of

Sèvres to hold good. To this the Turks agreed, but the Greeks refused, and so matters were left as they were, the Greeks soon afterwards commencing a new offensive. Mustapha Kemal was now fully convinced that all negotiations with the Allies were futile, and on the 21st March, concluded a definite treaty with the Moscow Soviet. On the following 18th of May, the Allies, exclusive of Greece, declared their neutrality in the war then existing between the Greeks and Turks.

On 10th July, 1921, the Greeks began their third offensive, but on 24th August, suffered a severe check on the Sakaria River, and on 16th September, began a general retreat, thus abandoning the project of reducing the interior of Asia Minor, and confining themselves to the maritime provinces already in their hands. In the course of the same month the French abandoned Cilicia, and left a large store of war material for the Turks. How far the French actually encouraged the Kemalists against the Greeks is not clear, but obviously they did not favour the formation of a Greek Empire in Asia Minor.

The Greeks now found themselves in a difficult position. M. Venizelos was no longer Premier and King Constantine had been invited back, but this did not mean the abandonment of the Imperialistic policy which had been fostered under Venizelos. By this time the Kemalist army had greatly increased in strength, and was better equipped, and showed every promise of being able to take up active operations against the Greeks, who now had to contemplate the possibility of being turned out of Asia altogether. On 15th February, 1922, the Greek minister, M. Gounaris, appealed to Lord Curzon, and it seems that Lord Curzon's reply encouraged him to hope that Great Britain would intervene if this worst eventuality came near. In March a new conference was held in Paris at which it was proposed that Smyrna, the chief city occupied by the Greeks, should be given back to the Turks, and the Treaty of Sèvres revised. To this the Geeks agreed on 23rd March, the government at Constantinople on 1st April, and the Angora government on 5th April, but this latter added the demand that Anatolia should be evacuated immediately, a demand to which the Greeks seemed willing to agree. But on 17th July, the Greek High Commissioner at Smyrna declared that the occupied territory when evacuated would not be handed back to the Turks, but would be recognised as an independent Republic of Ionia, under Greek protection; and on 29th July, the Greeks informed the Allies that it was their intention to occupy Constantinople. No doubt it was extremely difficult for King Constantine and his ministers to tell the Greeks that their high ambitions for which already great sacrifices had been made, were hopeless: but they would not have ventured to commit themselves so far unless confident in the support of the Allies who, in this case, meant Great Britain, for Italy had stated her determination to stand aloof, and France had shown herself disposed to assist the Turks.

On 4th August, Mr. Lloyd George made a very strong pro-Greek speech, which proved the immediate cause of the final disaster. No doubt it was intended to encourage the Greeks, but its more important result was to convince Mustapha Kemal that Great Britain was unwilling to press the Greeks to evacuate Anatolia as had been agreed at the Paris Conference in March, and so he resolved to force this evacuation forthwith. He began moving against the Greeks on 26th August. On 30th August, Smyrna fell, and the Greeks lost their last hope of an Asiatic Empire. An armistice was concluded between Greece and Angora on 11th October.

The Angora government had now showed plainly that it was prepared to resist the Allies in their Turkish policy, and quite able to hold its own : very clearly the whole of the Turkish people, in Europe as well as in Asia, was behind it, and the Muslim community throughout the whole world looked to it as a bulwark against western aggression. The war had greatly lowered the prestige of the western powers, and it is a mistake to suppose that the Allies, because victors in the west, were regarded with respect and awe. Their precarious position during the years, 1914-1916, was well known, and had been brought home to the East by the lavish bribes paid out by Great Britain, and the frantic efforts to win Asiatic support. The generation which remembered the intrigues and bribery of the war period could not possibly regard its suitor as so superbly formidable as had been assumed in times past. The post-war policy down to the unlucky Treaty of Sèvres had disclosed a boundless rapacity and lack of scruple, and Islam seemed to be the worst victim of the victors' dishonesty. But now, apparently, the tide had turned and the proud victors must sink that the victims might rise in their turn, in accordance with the teaching of Muslim theology which holds that power and greatness come to each nation in turn and, the more ruthlessly these are used, the more quickly the turn passes to the next so that, in accordance with the decrees of Divine justice, the proud are debased that they may learn that they are but God's creatures, and the oppressed are exalted to prosperity which is designed to compensate them for their sufferings. Already the Bolsheviki had shown that the power of the Allies was limited, and now Mustapha Kemal had given ground to hope that the long years during which Islam had been sinking before her opponents had at last come to an end, and it was her turn to mount upwards to success whilst the Western nations began their decline.

It was obvious that the Turks of Constantinople and Thrace were ardently attached to Mustapha Kemal, and in their loyalty to Angora found once more a racial solidarity which revived the Turkey of times long past. The Sultan Muhammad no longer ventured to stay in Constantinople and fled on a British ship to Malta. The National Assembly at Angora declared itself the true Turkish government and proclaimed the Sultan's desposition. No new Sultan was elected, and the Angora government took a Republican form; perhaps this had been agreed upon in the negotiations with the Moscow Soviet, at any rate, it was the most convenient course at the moment. The office of Khalif was separated from that of Sultan and Abdu l-Majid was elected to discharge whatever functions necessitated a " successor " of the Prophet as Commander of the Faithful, as heir of the relics of the Prophet, and as claimant to the guardianship of the holy cities. How far this office can rightly be regarded as " spiritual " is doubtful: if it be true that the Khalif is necessary as controller of the holy cities and protector of the pilgrimage we might perhaps more accurately describe him as temporal protector of religious privileges. It remains to be seen how far it is possible for him to act thus as a temporal guardian when he is no longer in command of temporal power.

The last month of 1922 was marked by a treaty between Angora and Afghanistan, an appropriate illustration of the way in which Islam was now disposed to rally to the one Muslim power which existed, not by the sufferance of the Western nations, but by its own vigour and efficiency. During the struggle Angora had allied itself with Moscow and the two had co-operated across Armenia, but this seems to have been purely a piece of temporary strategy and Angora has given no sign of enthusiasm for Communistic principles. At the moment the Turks regard Great Britain as their chief adversary because Great Britain was behind the Greek enterprise and she is supporting the King of the Hijaz who figures as the anti-Khalif. Recent events, however, have showed that the British government is by no means prepared to make sacrifices to maintain the Hijazi kingdom, and without British support, its position is extremely precarious. No doubt Angora is at present watching to see how far Great Britain will go to defend the Hijaz. Ibn Saʻud seems to have reached the conclusion that nothing will be done and that he is free to act as he sees fit without any reason to anticipate British interference, though possibly Great Britain would not allow the Hijazi kingdom to be removed altogether.

When the Turks evacuated Madina in the course of the war they removed certain relics, really of no great importance, from the tomb of the Prophet claiming that, as the Khalif was the rightful guardian of the holy sites, these sacred objects were to be held in trust by him and must not be allowed to fall into the hands of any other ruler. Early in 1923, the British government tried to negotiate the return of these relics, but so far Angora has refused. It touches, of course, the main point at issue—is the King of the Hijaz or the Khalif the rightful guardian of the holy cities? Does that guardianship itself carry the Khalifate with it?—Suppose the guardianship belongs to a purely "spiritual" Khalif, does that control interfere with the territorial jurisdiction of the King of the Hijaz, or does it only imply the oversight and control of the pilgrimage and the securing of facilities for it ? So far the British government has most carefully avoided any recognition of the King of the Hijaz as Khalif, he has called himself " Commander of the Faithful," but the title has never been used in any document officially issued by the British government. Islam has hardly appreciated the punctilious care with which the British have avoided any direct interference with the Khalifate, and so is now in no way committeed to oppose a spiritual Khalif, but the exact scope of that " spiritual " has yet to be made clear. Undoubtedly the family of the Sharif of Mecca is unpopular in Islam by reason of its notorious exactions from the pilgrims and the Meccans generally are regarded as more or less scandalous in their lives. No doubt the charges of laxity in religious observance and of immorality are true, as such charges are true of the residents in every holy place which is frequented by large pilgrimages, they are not peculiar to Mecca or to the sanctuaries of Islam. Probably those who, like the pilgrims, are passing through deep religious experiences are more profoundly shocked than they would be at other times or in other cities, whilst the regular residents about the sanctuary show the contempt proverbially bred of familiarity. Besides this there is the peculiar kinship between deep religious emotion and moral laxity, an undeniable phenomenon of psychology which does not seem ever to have been fully investigated. Anyhow, Islam at large has shown clearly that it does not intend to recognise the King of the Hijaz as Khalif and resents his present control of the holy cities regarding him merely as a political puppet set up by Great Britain as a means of manipulating Islam.

We must now turn to the war and post-war history of events in Egypt and India which show Nationalist movements of a simpler kind, their simpler character depending on their isolation from the real centre of Muslim politics so that they become more complex and serious as they are drawn into contact with the problem of the Khalifate. Thus it seems that the key of the future probably is at Angora, excluding, of course, the area of Wahhabi influence which has a possible menace for the Khalifate.

When war was declared in August, 1914, the Khedive, 'Abbas Hilmi, was at Constantinople, and when Turkey joined the Central Powers he accepted a post in the Turkish army. Meanwhile the government of Egypt was continued under the Regent who had been appointed to act during the Khedive's absence. At first the Turks' proclamation of a *jihad* caused a certain amount of disturbance in Egypt, and there was a good deal of anxiety as to what would happen, but as the British decided to use Egypt as a military base it soon became a huge camp, and in face of such vast military resources there was no effort even to whisper protest, indeed the quiet submissiveness was such that the British authorities formed an incorrect estimate of the peaceable and satisfied condition of the country and supposed that no resistance would be offered, no matter how great the provocation. On 18th

December, 1914, a British protectorate over the country was proclaimed, the Khedive was deposed and Husayn, his cousin, was declared his successor with the title of Sultan. This proctectorate was accepted without protest: it was felt to be a necessary war measure and it was generally understood that it would be no more than temporary. Amongst the people, however, the deposition of the Khedive was resented and Sultan Husayn had resason to fear the possibility of assassination so that elaborate preacutions were taken whenever he travelled about the country. Hitherto he had lived in retirement, but as he became better known he won a considerable measure of respect and personal popularity.

Early in the next year the Turks made an attack upon the Suez Canal, but the new disposition of forces arranged by Lord Kitchener, who paid a hasty visit to the country, enabled this to be countered. The Turkish attack, however, continued until the winter of 1916, when their repulse at al-'Arish caused them finally to abandon the attempt. On Christmas Day, 1916, scouting was going on to discover the whereabouts of the Turks, and next day it was known for certain that they were in full retreat upon Palestine.

During all this time when Egypt was beset by the Turks in the east and, at least up to the summer of 1916, by the Sanusi in the west, the country remained passive. It is said that, in the early days of the war, Egypt had offered to take a more active part and had desired to serve with the

British, but the offer had been somewhat contemptuously rejected: certainly Egyptian artillery had taken an active, and very creditable part, in the repulse of the Turks from the Canal. Yet for all this there were indications of unfriendly feelings beneath, where such feelings could be safely shown. The writer remembers instances in the neighbourhood of Deirut where this took the form of abuse of Christians called out where an intervening canal offered a position of security and the hearers were not supposed to understand the words used, and there was very definitely shown dislike in some of the slum districts of Cairo and Bulaq. It must be admitted also that the attitude of the army of occupation rather tended to exasperate these feelings. As the war went on, many of those who received commissions were drawn from material which differed from that which had furnished commissioned officers in pre-war days: most of these no doubt gave an excellent account of themselves in the performance of their military duties, but they, and still more the Colonial officers, very often had the more brusque and aggressive tone which is rather cultivated in modern business life and, coming from narrower and more provincial surroundings, they were less able to appreciate and understand the entirely new conditions in which they found themselves placed. Unquestionably the personnel of the British forces in Egypt during the war caused a great change of feeling in the country which acted unfavourably towards the British.

The death of Sultan Husayn, who had gradually gathered a certain measure of respect and esteem, on 9th October, 1917, was a great loss to the influence of the British as his successor, the Sultan Ahmad Fuad, never acquired either popularity or respect. Indeed the winter of 1917-1918, marked the spread of a very much more pronounced anti-British feeling than had existed at any previous time. This was largely connected with the Egyptian Labour Corps, and the condition of service therein. That had been raised as an auxiliary body first in 1915 for service in Gallipoli, and had then been continued for service in Egypt and along the route to Palestine. At first there was a ready response and recruits came in freely as the pay offered was not merely good but lavish, whilst the engagement was a contract for a year under civilian conditions. As the Corps was working in conjunction with the army it was, of course, inevitable that it came sometimes under military discipline and this was not consistent with the civilian conditions of the contract : sometimes those whose term of service had expired were not allowed to go home at once, and it was said there were cases where death took place and the relatives at home were not informed, all unfortunate, but inevitable incidents : worst of all the Corps frequently came under fire and conditions during the advance into Palestine in 1917-1918 were, it will be remembered, fairly serious. Under these circumstances it is not altogether surprising that in the winter, 1917-1918, and during the year, 1918, it became difficult to obtain voluntary recruits for the Corps; but men were badly wanted and pressure was put upon the local authorities to keep up the supply with the inevitable result that the village officials were driven to use compulsion, and obtained men by a species of press-gang which worked far more harshly than the regular conscription of the Egyptian army and often brought in men who had already obtained exemption from military service, sometimes this proved a convenient means of getting rid of persons who were personally disliked by the village omdah, and in any case popular opinion considered that the conscripts were taken to fight for a foreign power in a quarrel which was not theirs. No doubt the British authorities were not directly responsible for the abuses which took place, but the nature of the abuses must have been fairly obvious to those who had any familiarity with oriental methods. Thus, by the latter part of 1918, the general feeling of the fellahin, who had been acquiescent or actively pro-British before the war, had developed a very intense anti-British character though, at the time, very few ventured to make any overt sign of their attitude.

The Armistice was declared on 11th November, 1918, and two days later Sa'ad Pasha Zaghlul and a few others called at the Residency in Cairo and asked that, as the war was now over, the protectorate which was professedly a temporary war measure might be terminated and the country allowed self-determination. This request was largely based on the declaration of President Wilson that the war was being fought in defence of the rights of small coun-

countries and for the purpose of securing them the right of determining their own form of government, but very much the same thing had been said by British ministers earlier in the war when they were freely making promises without any clear realization of their future effect and hardly expecting, perhaps, that they would ever be in a position to redeem them. Zaghlul's request was, under the circumstances, reasonable, but the authorities in Cairo were not, of course, in a position to grant it at their own discretion. Perhaps the manner in which the refusal was made was rather high-handed and lacking in tact, but at the time it was not supposed that the Nationalists were more than a negligible minority. Zaghlul's further request to be allowed to go to England in order to plead the Nationalist cause was peremptorily refused and this undoubtedly was a serious error, which was made worse by the exclusion of Egypt from the Peace Conference. It was an error, for Egypt had definitely been declared free from Turkey, its previous over-lord, and if this freedom did not mean independence, the only alternative was that Egypt was now regarded as a part of the British Empire in spite of the plain statement that the protectorate was only a war measure. But the protectorate continued, and Egypt found itself liberated from the very slight bond which bound it to Turkey, but reduced to a very much more subordinate position under Great Britain. Theoretically the British attitude was indefensible and when the Peace Conference ratified the protectorate no unprejudiced observer could find any plausible excuse.

Should Great Britain have recognised the independence of Egypt ? Theoretically, yes ; but in the name of humanity and practical expediency, no—as the country was not ready and neither life nor property would have been safe. It is an instance of one of those insoluble knots in which all theoretical justice and right must be violated for justice sake. The making of rash promises of " self determination," whilst the war was still in progress was criminal, the giving of pledges by those who did not realize the risk involved in carrying them out because they had no intimate knowledge of the country or its inhabitants, was equally criminal ; the refusal to permit Zaghlul or any other body of citizens to plead their case in person was an error, and the exclusion of Egypt from the Peace Conference was also an error. It might have been admitted that the protectorate was now terminated and devolution working towards autonomy might proceed, although for some time to come, under the peculiar circumstances produced by the process of recovery from war and the difficulty of readjustment, the change would have to work gradually and some time might elapse before complete independence could take effect, it being plainly understood that its delay and any other measure of control was purely temporary and intended only to help the country to pass through a difficult period during which Great Britain had to make provision for her own future safety. But the victorious Allies in 1919 were suffering from a kind of intoxication. The Peace Conference seemed to suppose that its mere will could dispose of nations and countries with a kind of divine authority and that earth contained no one who would venture to question its wishes.

The Egyptian nationalists gave very free expression to their resentment encouraged by the impunity with which the British government usually allowed the most outspoken criticism, but the British still regarded their complaints as expressing only the feelings of a trivial and negligible minority. On the 9th March, 1919, Sa‘ad Pasha Zaghlul and nine others were arrested and deported to Malta, and it was expected that before this firm attitude the disaffected would no longer venture on an open expression of their feelings. The result, however, was widely different from this expectation and surprised both the British authorities and the nationalist leaders. At once riots broke out in Cairo, daily increasing in violence, and quickly spread to Lower Egypt and then, on March 15th to Upper Egypt: telegraph wires were pulled down, railway lines torn up, and in many places the Europeans closely besieged in their dwellings: in a few cases the Turkish flag was set up and Turkish suzerainty proclaimed. Then, on March 17th, came the atrocious murder of English officers on the train at Deirut. By the middle of April the authorities were able to report that all was quiet again, but the intervening experience had entirely changed the attitude of Great Britain towards Egypt and had disclosed facts of an unexpected nature. In the first place, the outbreak was far more general than had been anticipated, no one had realised how wide-spread and how strong was the anti-British feeling in the country and how fallacious the appearance of quiet obedience : it had not been usual to regard the Egyptians as a warlike people, which normally they are not, though they are not one of those degenerate races which are unable or unwilling to undertake military service, but over and over again in the course of mediæval and modern history the Egyptians have suddenly shown soldierly possibilities which are by no means contemptible. Still more unexpected and serious was the revelation that the fellahin, who had been generally regarded as the steady supporters of the British rule, were thoroughly disaffected : this was the most discouraging experience, as it completely undermined the moral position of the British rulers. It was the result, no doubt, of the injustice of the conscription made for the Egyptian Labour Corps, for which the British were supposed responsible, and of the hardship caused by the commandeering of beasts of burden for which compensation was paid, but for whose loss compensation could not make good. Behind this was the half-formed discontent due to the radical change taking place in social conditions as the peasant proprietorship of the older fellahin was replaced by the latifunda due to the introduction of cotton and sugar, changes brought about by the extended irrigation and making for the greater prosperity and increased population of the country. but causing the older cultivators to be replaced by hired labourers. Most of all the ferocity of the mob in the outbreaks was an unexpected quality, though in fact it should not have been so, as it is the perfectly natural outcome of the hysterical element which is in the Egyptian and of which indications must have been apparent to every thoughtful observer.

From the time of the outbreak in 1919 to the present, negotiations have been going on for the provision of self-government in Egypt. It is hardly necessary to follow them in detail. The nationalists have driven home and emphasized their points by a series of strikes, demonstrations, and such like, whilst the British, now fully aware of the serious determination of the people to secure their independence, have made concessions and drafted a scheme of government which grants all the main points demanded. The general moral is by no means gratifying to the British. Apparently they have been compelled to give in by the determined attitude of the people, and they are commonly regarded as blustering bullies who will at once abate their pretensions when faced firmly—a very unhappy result for the prestige of Great Britain and for the Egyptians themselves, who stand to lose much if the ties of sympathy and co-operation between England and Egypt are relaxed. That the efforts made by Great Britain since 1919 are conscientious and practical is hardly recognised : the superficial impression is that the British government will shrink before violence whilst it refuses to listen to justice and this is bound to bear its fruit in armies and violence for many years to come. Egypt does not realise that in 1919 England was suffering from a kind of *dementia* due to the intoxication of victory and has since been making its way back to recovery and sanity.

Another interesting side-light on the course of events in Egypt arises when we note that Sa'ad Pasha Zaghlul and his chief supporters have been willing to meet the terms proposed by the British, but have been denounced and opposed for this by their own followers. Apparently their is a split in the nationalist ranks and Zaghlul is not anxious to commit himself to the extreme section. Now here it is quite possible to read between the lines. It seems fairly certain that the Bolsheviki have tried to encourage disorder in Egypt. How far their efforts have been successful it is impossible to say at present : certainly there has been an increased production of Arabic translations of works by Tolstoi and Russian socialists—though not, apparently, of actual communist treatises. No doubt there is a Bolshevik section, and no doubt, now that the real tendencies and aims of Bolshevism have been disclosed, as was done in 1920, the nationalist leaders such as Zaghlul, are thoroughly shy of those extremists and strongly inclined to co-operate with the

British against Bolshevism. If this be so, their tendency must be to some measure reactionary and so disposed to make terms with the British, and thus the case seems to stand at the present moment.

Events in India have followed rather different lines. In 1914-1915 there was a great impetus towards nationalism, and in 1916 Lord Hardinge, the Viceroy, made promises of certain concessions. In 1917 the Secretary of State for India, Mr. Montague, visited the country to make enquiries as to the details of what was desired and what was practicable, and his report, presented in 1918, advised considerable concessions which were embodied in a law of the following year. Before this appeared, however, came the very dark experience of 1918 with riots through all northern India, probably stirred up by Bolshevik agents, and difficulties on the Afghan frontier, so that it seemed doubtful whether matters could be left much in Indian hands for the present. Very soon, therefore, followed the Rowlatt Bill which gave the authorities power to extend war measures and restrictions where these were judged necessary, and this was followed by violent outbreaks in the Panjab and in the North-West and West. All these, however, rather concern the domestic history of India than the community of Islam. As the acute sufferings of 1919 passed away leaving, unfortunately, very sore feelings behind, the Muslims of India began to be drawn gradually into touch with the aspirations and grievances of the Turks as expressed at Angora and thus arose what is known as the Khalifate movement in India. It is quite possible to prove that that movement is a manufactured one, and to refute its pretensions; the constitutional history of the Khalifate is involved and obscure, and almost any theory which may be brought forward can be refuted by citing some divergent theory. But after all, the theories of constitutional and canon law are but attempts to express in philosophical language the realities of social relations, and those relations, in a living community, are not always capable of reduction to perfectly logical terms : real life is full of inconsistencies and contradictions, and it is theory which has to be re-expressed to keep in touch with facts. The truth is that Islam, for more than a century past, has found itself fighting a losing battle in its older territory, though more than compensaing for this by missionary work in newer areas. But the traditional position of Islam is that of an independent church and not simply of a religion, whilst the trend of political change has been detrimental to that ecclesiastical status and Islam has hardly yet found itself able to realise the more spiritual and non-ecclesiastical position. After the war Islam seemed to be faced with complete and final ruin as an independent and self-governing church, and has very naturally thrown itself in with the policy of the one branch which has shown itself willing and able to defend the traditional status, and, if this involves the negation of principles held by the canonists, those principles must go. The Khalifate will be maintained in defiance of every theory if needs be, and by those whose own sectarian views deny the need of a Khalifate, if that office is maintained by a vigorous and efficient power which seems likely to make it the nucleus of a renascent Islam, and that to-day seems to be the promise held out by Angora.

At the moment the world of Islam is most anxious about the political position and the threatened world-wide supremacy of the western powers, and under the influence of this anxiety it is ready to make alliance with Bolshevism or anything else which can be played off against the west. In this attitude unquestionably Islam is mistaken. The entirely erroneous idea that the western powers are animated by a Crusading spirit is fallacious in the extreme, and is likely to direct attention in quite the wrong direction. The west is influenced by no zeal for Christianity, by no hostility to Islam, but simply by the pursuit of material gain which is as hostile to Christianity as to Islam :: the acts detrimental to Muslim interests which have been resented are simply due to the fact that in some cases Islam happens to stand in the way of certain commercial enterprises. This does not mean that Muslims are wrong in regarding western progress with misgiving : in reality that progress is even more menacing than they suppose, though it is working, not for the triumph of Christianity but for sheer materialism. The political advance of the Powers of Europe is less dangerous than the undermining of Muslim communities by scepticism and materialism, and this is very certainly in progress. One of the most serious symptoms of this undermining is the steady decline in the numbers of those taking part in the annual pilgrimage which, as we have noted, is the thing which more than all else binds together the world of Islam. The anxiety caused by this decline has been the most active cause of the stirring of the Arabs in the Hijaz who have supposed (wrongly) that the pilgrimage could be made more attractive if freed from Turkish control, and they are, of course, most vitally affected by its decline. That Islam is now at a very critical turning-point is unquestionable, and events in the Hijaz have simply precipitated the crisis. The most significant other event is the steady, though unostentatious, rise of a sect of Islam which needs no Khalif, the puritan sect of the Wahhabis which, within its own sphere, is as strong as the Khalifate of Angora, perhaps stronger, and seems to be steadily gaining whilst having the experience of mingled loss and gain. The British, misled by Indian phases of Wahhabism, are inclined to regard Ibn Sa'ud's kingdom with suspicion, but it certainly is at the moment the most efficient Muslim power and is itself friendly disposed towards Great Britain—as yet it has no direct contact with any other European power: the only doubt is whether that kingdom will survive its present ruler.

At this critical juncture it is indeed doubtful which of the possible cross-roads Islam will take but both Christian and Muslim should remember that they are not so much antagonists pitted against one another, as alike threatened by a more sinister adversary which is hostile to all religion, whose victory would be facilitated by strife too vigorously carried out between the two religions which share so large a part of the civilized world.

INDEX

'Abbas Hilmi, 200
'Abdu l-Hamid, 121, etc.; 158
Afghan envoy to Moscow, 87
Afghanistan, 176
    treaty with Angora, 197
Africa partitioned, 59-60, 86
Agricultural basis of Asiatic society, 83
Ahmadiya, 99, etc.
    teaching, 105
Ahmed Fuad, Sultan (then King) of Egypt, 203
'Ali, 10, 11, etc.
Amanullah Amir of Afghanistan, 178, 186
Angora government, 192, 195, etc.
    becomes a republic, 197
Arab nationalism, 134, etc.; 137
Arabi Pasha, 124, 141-2
Arabia, 1
Armistice of 1918, 204
" Authority " in religion, 17
Azalis, 116
Azerbaijan Republic, 180, 182

Bab, 111, etc.
Babists founded, 111
    persecuted, 113-4
Baghdad, 16
Baha'i sect, 115, etc.
Baha'ullah, 114, 116
Baku Soviet, 182
    occupied by Bolsheviki, 185
    Congress, 186
Balkan War, 55, 130
Berlin Congress of 1919, 185
Biyadiyya, 49
Bolshevik influence in Egypt, 201
    policy in Asia, 171, etc.
British Indian Association, 96
    rule in Egypt, 144-5
Browne, Prof., 115-6
Burckhardt, 34

" Capitulations," 141-2
Castagne: *Bolchevisme et l'Islam*, 181
Chicago branch of Baha'i sect, 117
Chirol, Sir Valentine, 96
Christians, fanaticism imputed to, 55, 61
    feeling against, 53
    influence on Islam, 3, 4
    missionaries, 56, etc.
" Committee of Union and Progress," 138
Courtesy, 80-83

Danfodio, 41-42
Deirut outrage, 207
Democracy, 78-80
Divorce, 67-76

Economic causes for disliking Europeans, 83
Education, Western ideas in, 62-67
Egypt, British occupation, 141, etc.; 145, 147
    during the War, 200, etc.
    excluded from Peace Conference, 206
Egyptian Labour Corps, 203, 208
    nationalism, 140
Egyptians anti-British, 148, 202, etc.
Enver Pasha, 157
Erzerum conference, 187

Family life, 76-78
Fanaticism imputed to Christians, 55, 61
Feisal, the Emir, 166, etc.
Financiers in control of Western governments, 85, 93

German reverence for efficiency, 154-6
    influence in Turkey, 133
Ghazna, 21
Greeks defeated, 193-4

Habibullah Amir of Afghanistan, 176-8
Hafiz Ibrahim, Egyptian poet, 148
Hakim Ajmal Haziqu l-Mulk, 98
Hakim Nuru d-Din, 102
Hellenistic influence, 14
Hijazi king, 26, 27, 39, 159, 162, etc.; 198, 199 (cf. Sharif of Mecca)
    kingdom, 139
Hijaz railway, 136

Ibadi sect, 12
Ibn Sa'ud, 36, 37, 39-41, 139, 160, 198
Ibn Taymiya 31, 80
Ikhwan of the Wahhabis, 40
India, 50, etc.; 211, etc.
    anti-British feeling in, 150, etc.
Indian loyalty, 152-3
    Mutiny, 149, 152
    nationalism, 149
Irreligion of Europeans, 61
Islam originally an Arab religion, 4-7
Islamji party, 128
Izvestia, 87, 179, 180

Jemal ad-Din, 123

Khalif, office of, 14, 60
    elected at Angora, 197
Khalifate decay of 19, 20
    movement in India, 212
Kharijites, 12
Khawal, 75

INDEX

Khedive, 39, 140
  deposed, 201
Khuda Bukhsh, 98
Khwajah Kamal ad-Din, 59, 103, 106
Kitchener, Lord, 201, 148

Lahore branch of the Ahmadiyya, 105-6
  mission, 103-4
  Muslim society, 98
Lloyd George, Mr., 195
London, Conference of, 192
Lucknow society, 99
  college, 99

Mahmud of Ghazna, 12
Mamluks of Egypt, 23
Marriage, 67-76
Mawlawi, 7
Mawlawi Chiragh 'Ali, 97
  Karamat 'Ali, 43
Mecca, guardianship of, 26, 160-161
Merchant route through Arabia, 2
Mesopotamia, 169
Mirza 'Ali Muhammad, 112
Mirza Ghulam Ahmad, 100, etc.
Moscow conference of 1920, 185
Mot'a marriage, 68
Mughul invasion, 22
Muhammad, 1, 2, 3, 4
  'Ali of Egypt, 34
  al-Muntazir, 10
Murabits, 30
Muslim conquests, reasons of, 5-6
Mustapha Kemal of Egypt, 146
Mustapha Kemal of Turkey, 188, etc.
M'tazilites, 16, 17, 18, 97

Nationalism, 125, etc.
Naturis, 97
Necharis, 97

Othmanli Turks, 23, 125

Palmerston, Lord, views on foreign investments, 88
Pan-Islamic ideas, 120, etc.
Panjab rising, 152
Pan-Turkish party, 127-8, 157
Peace conference, 166
Persia, 170, etc.; 176, 183
  partitioned, 52
Persian period, 9, 15
Philby, *Heart of Arabia*, 37, 49
Pilgrimage, importance of, 28
  of 1916, 164
Political objections to Europeans, 90-94
Polygamy, 67, etc.

Qadian branch of the Ahmadiya, 103-4
  college at, 104

Quraysh, Khalif must be of, 26

Race and colour question, 88-90
Rafi-yadaym, 43
Revolution of 1908 in Turkey, 125, 126, 138
Riyadh, 35
Rowlatt Bill, 211
Russian revolution, 169

Saint worship, 29-30, 31
San Remo, "Supreme Council," 191
Sanusi, 44, etc.; 201
Sayyid Ahmed Khan, 95, etc.
  Ahmed Shah, 42-43
  Amir Ali, 97
  Murtada, 80
Semitic migrations, 3
"Seveners," 11
Sevres, treaty of, 191-3, 196
Sharif of Mecca, 37, 158-9, 160, 199
  (cf. Hijazi king)
Shi'ites, 10, 15, 110, etc.
Smyrna taken by the Turks, 194
Subh-i-Azel, 113, 115
Sultan's claim to Khalifate, 23, 24
Sykes-Picot agreement, 160
Syria anti-Turk, 136
Syrian expedition, 165, 168-9

Ta'aiyuni, 44
Tashkend Soviet, 170, 172, 175
  University, 175
Tekin Alp, 128
Townsend, Meredith, 82-3, 148
Tripoli, 46-47, 131
Tughril, 22
Turkey, 51
Turkish period, 9, 19, 21, etc.; 29
  nationalism, 125, etc.
Turks become anti-British, 132-4
  join Germany, 157
"Twelvers," 10, 111

'Ulema, 13, 24, 25
'Umar, 6
'Umayyad Khalifs, 8, etc.

Wahhabis, 13
  origin, 31, 32
  early spread, 33
  checked, 34, 35
  revival, 35, etc.
  British dislike of, 44, 214
  in India, 42
  in the Sudan, 41 (cf. Ibn Sa'ud)
Woking mosque at, 106
Women, position of, 72, etc.

Young Egyptian party, 147
Young Turk party, 120, etc.; 131

Zaghlul, 204, 205, 207, 210
Zaydites, 11